"*Missing Time* is distinctive for the fresh, new interpretations of familiar subjects to be found in its pages. This is cultural criticism at its originating best."

— *Vivian Gornick*

"In these wry, funny, and incisive essays on topics ranging from growing up with *The X-Files*, to feeling disappointed in Philip Roth, to what we might learn from second-generation US communists, Ari M. Brostoff helps us diagnose and historicize our present in a way beautifully true to the legacy of '70s feminist writing and also to the 'political life of diaspora Jewry and all it [stands] for: ambivalence, absurdism, emasculation.'"

— *Sianne Ngai*

"At a moment when so many radicals are stuck in and with images of a long-ago past—the New Deal, Reconstruction, Weimar—Ari M. Brostoff offers the left the 'unfamiliar sense of living in our own time.' With a lyricism and density that recalls the most daring writing of Ellen Willis, Brostoff has built, in these essays, a world of fantasy and fear, of hunger and loneliness, that looks and feels very much like the present."

— *Corey Robin*

"Few books come close to relaying the sense of ruptured time and lost dreams that have haunted the American left—queer and feminist, Jewish and critical. This one chronicles with exactitude falling in love and with politics, the oscillations of enchantment and hope. Luckily for us, the dream keeps emerging for a Jewish displacement of the Zionist ideal, the reanimation of communism, and the compelling promise of the Bernie burn for socialism among feminist allies. Even when we have lost hope altogether, there is apparently still a way to canvass popular culture, collect the arcana, read Philip Roth and Vivian Gornick again, tell the story of one's childhood friendships to bring about flashes of improbable hope, pressing upon the traces of the holy to emit their light. Ari M. Brostoff gives us a lucid sense of the arc of hope and despair as it passes through popular culture, electoral politics, and the endless repetitions of family romances gone sour. The radical hope never shakes its despair, but neither does it succumb. The writing moves in and against despair to find the promise of diaspora and the prospect of living well outside the nationalist fix of the homeland and its violences—and to cultivate a queer socialism wrought from the rough-edged fragments of the everyday."

   —*Judith Butler*

"Who says that communism doesn't belong intimately to the present? In these deft essays, Ari M. Brostoff thinks about the urgency and untimeliness of a communist politics and finds it in evidence everywhere: in the post–cold war paranoias of *The X-Files*, the fever dreams that fuel today's nascent fascisms, the capacious family portraits of Vivian Gornick. *Missing Time* argues vigorously in favor of thinking about the palpably communal stakes of private fantasy, as if our collective psychodramas could summon political forces we only kind of understand. Brostoff's keen method is to take feeling seriously, without fully believing in it, and the result is an exercise in learning how to think about the conjuncture, make sense of its bewildering patterns, and determine—as 'body snatchers, homosexuals, Jews,' and everyone else—what to do next."

—*Kay Gabriel*

"Ari M. Brostoff is changing the terms of conversation on the left. They know exactly which diasporic figures to return to wider public discourse, and which to let our grip loosen on. Along the way, we get a beautiful, accidental trans memoir that organically folds questions of sex and gender into a story about political transformation more broadly. This book is a beacon, creating new political idioms that seem familiar—but which transform under Brostoff's prismatic language and rare sensibility. *Missing Time* is serious, considered, and crucial analysis delivered with a spry, addictive touch."

—*Jordy Rosenberg*

"Ari M. Brostoff is a world-saving firecracker of a critic—sparks, danger, surprise, illusion, enchantment, escape, redemption. Their voice, comic and austere, pared down, purveys all the merciless sharpness of Didion but with new wild forgiving zones of application, as if Brostoff were floating the hope that wit could repair our ruined time. This magnificent book, *Missing Time*, a strange taut gem, portends a future I want to follow, a future that will instruct me on how to see chaos clearly."

— *Wayne Koestenbaum*

"Ari M. Brostoff writes like a charming stranger; I always feel we must have met before. One reads these essays with the mounting sense that dialectical materialism, for all its pretensions at science, is in fact a kind of mysticism, even a Jewish one. This is true not because history is unreal but because it has made itself available to us primarily through ritual, fantasy, television, public protest, private longing, and forty years of wandering in the desert. Brostoff does not believe in God, but they do believe unabashedly in belief; in their holy of holies, one finds only hastily written directions to the next tabernacle. *Missing Time* teaches us that even the revolution, hoped for and given up and hoped for again, may be a travesty, in the old sense of cross-dressing—the experimental, often precarious assumption of a style that has not yet found a form and which nevertheless can bring to some of us, in flashes of messianic time, the closest thing we have ever known to joy."

— *Andrea Long Chu*

MISSING TIME

P.S. 1 Symposium: A Practical Avant-Garde

What We Should Have Known: Two Discussions

What Was the Hipster? A Sociological Investigation

The Trouble Is the Banks: Letters to Wall Street

No Regrets: Three Discussions

Buzz: A Play

Other Russias

Canon/Archive: Studies in Quantitative Formalism

The Earth Dies Streaming: Film Writing, 2002–2018

MISSING TIME

ESSAYS

ARI M. BROSTOFF

ⴖ+1 BOOKS

ⴖ+1 FOUNDATION   NEW YORK

Published 2022 by n+1 Foundation

37 Greenpoint Avenue #316, Mailbox 18

Brooklyn, New York 11222

www.nplusonemag.com

ISBN 978-1-953813-04-6

Printed by the Sheridan Press

Manufactured in the United States of America

Design by Rachel Ossip

First Printing

The n+1 Foundation's programs are made possible in part by the New York State Council on the Arts with the support of the Office of the Governor and the New York State Legislature, as well as by public funds from the New York City Department of Cultural Affairs, in partnership with the City Council.

For my friends

CONTENTS

If nothing happens it is possible
To make things happen.

— Jack Spicer, "A Postscript for Charles Olson"

INTRODUCTION

AROUND THE START OF 2016, I GOT IT INTO MY HEAD THAT what I needed was a break from time.

The facts of the situation were banal. I had been in graduate school in New York for several years and could not afford my rent. I wanted to move to a place where I could live cheaply and quietly and finish my dissertation quickly before I had to start teaching again, so I sublet my room in Brooklyn and took one in a less expensive college town nearby, hoping to transform a sense of entrapment in a strangled industry into a more romantic vision of isolated productivity. I felt I needed a recess from my life, and from life in general, so that I would have time to do nothing but work.

I wasn't the only one trying to effect a temporal rupture. The would-be Democratic presidential candidate Bernie Sanders and the movement around him had cracked something open in the American political firmament, upsetting a fragile coalition of assumptions that held together a sense of the historical present. Sanders appeared to be an ambassador from a lost civilization of the 20th century. His campaign proposed a more radical break from time than the one I had attempted: not an individual time-out but a collective resetting of clocks, a strike against the forces that had locked working people out of history for decades.

Both plans—my small one and the Bernie campaign's large one—seemed briefly like they might succeed. I set up the schedule that had eluded me in the city, walking each morning to the campus library, where I had my own shelf in an ornate uninhabited reading room, and coming home in the evening to the dingy apartment I shared with two strangers. It was restorative to have some time alone, and I became bloated with ideas. I hoped my research would help me understand the forces that, sometime in the 1970s, had ushered out an interval of utopian aspirations for the left and ushered in what the feminist literary critic Jane Elliott called "static time": a period in which life dragged on but hope faded away.

Then, a kind of madness set in. During previous stretches of depression and anxiety, I had experienced the world as overstimulating, as though it wished to voice a complaint: electrical grids too loud, lights too bright and the wrong color, water that turned salty in my mouth. This time, it seemed the world had stopped speaking to me at all. Anything that broke through felt like a violation. (The horn section on *Lemonade* was a particular issue.) I tried to suck the life out of books as efficiently as possible but got little done, as though I were riding a bicycle in place. Bernie passed through town once and I watched him speak from across a vast public square, attempting to stay connected to the possibility of change.

In the months that followed, I became paralyzed by the task of choosing between equally bad options for what to do next. Hillary Clinton won the Democratic primary, suggesting that things would go on much as they had. But by this point, I had become detached from events beyond my shrunken life. In June, a shooter killed dozens of people at a gay nightclub in Orlando; in July, police murdered a Black man named Philando Castile at a traffic stop in Minnesota. The scenes of collective mourning and protest that on other occasions had made such events unbearably real, if incommensurably distant, had receded from my field of vision. Life in New York went on without me and I stopped wanting to visit. I could not remember why it was that anyone wanted to live anywhere.

It seemed that, having exited time, I could not get back in; I began to suspect I had never been part of its flow at all. Nor could I recall what it was about the past that had led me from the city to the library to begin with. In the 1930s, the Marxist critic and Jewish theologian Walter Benjamin diagnosed an ailment he called left-wing melancholy. Benjamin was a professed melancholic himself who once described his moods of indecision and withdrawal as born of an overwhelming sense of historical longing: he imagined himself as a "ragpicker . . . at the dawn of the day of the revolution," sifting through the lost and forgotten past in search of something to redeem. But a different flavor of despondence, he wrote in a scathing 1931 essay, had set in among the irony-poisoned bourgeois German leftists of the Weimar years. Benjamin pilloried these contemporaries for opting out of the political demands of the moment altogether and attaching themselves spitefully to their losses like "a man who yields himself up entirely to the inscrutable accidents of his digestion." Apprehending my own melancholia, I sensed how quickly one could slip from one version of Benjamin's ailment to the other, how easily political heartbreak could calcify into narcissistic bitterness.

In the decades following the end of the cold war, many thinkers on the left followed Benjamin in theorizing the connection between radical politics and melancholia, an affect that—as the scholar Enzo Traverso put it in a 2016 study—had become "the dominant feeling of a world burdened with its past, without a visible future." In an influential 1999 essay, the political theorist Wendy Brown connected Benjamin's critique of left-wing melancholy to a distinction Sigmund Freud made between mourning and melancholy. For Freud, a subject experienced mourning when they grieved the loss of something or someone they were attached to. They experienced melancholy, on the other hand, when they were unable to grieve such a loss, because they could not—or would not—acknowledge that the beloved object was really gone. What was it, Brown asked, that contemporary leftists could not mourn because they could not admit they'd lost it to begin with?

I spent the summer in the library numbly trying to figure out what I was refusing to mourn, and becoming alarmed every time I got too close to an answer. Finally, that August, a friend called me back to

Brooklyn to watch his cats for a month, and I stumbled home. I was still shaky when Donald Trump won the election a few months later. I did not see it coming; I was horrified and stunned. Yet almost immediately, as the liberal consensus began to implode and the old choice between socialism and barbarism reasserted itself without apologies, the world came back into hideous focus and I felt, maybe for the first time, like a long-term inhabitant of the present.

THE ESSAYS IN THIS BOOK were written between early 2016, just before my break from time, and early 2020, after the outbreak of the pandemic but before the brief, electrifying Black-led uprising that flung open the doors to the possibility of life beyond the police state. They often reach back into the 20th century, to settings and figures I had been thinking about for a long time: the everyday life of the American Communist Party, the politics of sexual liberation, Philip Roth, David Duchovny, the Los Angeles suburbs of my childhood. But they also constitute a sort of diary of the frenetic, absurd, often devastating, sometimes astonishing period in which they were completed and first published. This is not simply because they deal with subjects all too present in the discourse of the past several years—Hillary Clinton's likability, Jeffrey Epstein's eugenic fantasies—but also because this period of upheaval fundamentally reordered my relationship to the past. History, notoriously, was said to have ended in the 1990s, when I was growing up. But, then, things changed.

The slow crumbling of American empire has ignited the historical imaginations of both radicals and fascists, who sometimes accuse each other, or antagonists within their own ranks, of engaging in cosplay. This may be simply the way things go in moments when the trapdoor to the political unconscious comes loose. Just as "the beginner who has learned a new language always translates it back into his mother tongue," as Karl Marx observed in "The Eighteenth Brumaire of Louis Napoleon," the course to revolution begins with dress-up: the French Revolution "draped itself" in the costume of ancient Rome, while the Revolution of 1848 "knew nothing better to do than to parody" the French Revolution in turn. With more practice, however, the revolutionary "assimilates the spirit of the new language and expresses himself freely in it," an achievement Marx likens to "the awakening of the dead." I remember how thrilling, but also how ridiculous, it felt at first to call people comrades; now it feels like we have always done so, and viewed at a different time scale, we have.

These essays, then, make up an idiosyncratic account of a shift that has taken place for many leftists over the past few years from an essentially backward-looking orientation to an unfamiliar sense of living in our own time. I was able to write about these 20th-century tableaux only once I could see myself on the same historical continuum as my subjects; then I could see that I existed and that they did, too. The first piece, "Where the Boys Are," takes its title from a comment by Gloria Steinem, who told an interviewer that young women were joining the Sanders campaign because the boys were doing it—part of a widespread dismissal of women on the left that was making me crazy. The essay travels from Bernie Sanders's ham-handed 1970s writing on sexual politics to the passion play of Monica Lewinsky in an attempt to under-stand the erasure of a feminist vision of women as political subjects driven by desire. The second piece, "Missing Time," tries to capture the vertigo induced by the return of buried political currents in the early Trump years. In that essay, I return to a stack of mid-dle school journals chronicling a foundational friend-ship and the political education I received from *The*

X-Files—a show that captured a moment when alien abduction, often described by alleged abductees as an experience of "missing time," was popularly invoked to explain widespread symptoms of trauma with no apparent explanation.

The last three essays in this collection turn increasingly toward Jewish cultural and political questions. I did not anticipate this turn—not because I had never written about Jewishness before, but because I had gotten myself into the habit of avoiding it as much as possible. The American Jewish establishment of the early 21st century did an impressive if ultimately unsustainable job of silencing political dissent within the organized Jewish community while domesticating and co-opting any traces of intellectual fervor or cultural experimentation to be found there. I grew up in a Jewish world that answered to this establishment and then, after college, worked as a journalist for Jewish publications that helped to manufacture consensus within it. These publications offered me serious training as a young reporter and critic. But I was chilled by the silence around the office at the liberal Zionist *Forward* during the 2008 war on Gaza, and crushed by the recklessness and cynicism at the online magazine *Tablet*, which subsequently moved far to the right. By the time I left for grad school, the link between Jewishness and writing had effectively been severed for me. I did not feel silenced, I just felt like I didn't have much to say.

In 2019, however, with some hesitation at first, I began working as an editor at *Jewish Currents*, a magazine as untimely as the contents of this book: it was started by Jewish Communists in 1946 and relaunched in 2018 by young Jewish leftists looking for a political, cultural, and intellectual home. Only one of these essays appeared in the magazine, but all were informed by this resurfacing. "The Double's Allegiance"—written shortly after the congresswoman Ilhan Omar was spuriously accused of suggesting that American Jews exhibited "dual loyalty"—centers on Philip Roth's madcap Israeli spy novel *Operation Shylock* and my own frustrated desire to enlist Roth as an anti-Zionist Jewish icon. "The Right Kind of Continuity," coauthored with Noah Kulwin, is an attempt to think through Jeffrey Epstein's plan to inseminate scores of women with his own DNA alongside his prominence within the Jewish philanthropic establishment, which dedicated itself for decades to the promotion of "Jewish continuity"—a biopolitical project aimed at the promotion of marriage and child-rearing within the organized Jewish community. Though it is the closest thing among these essays to a piece of straightforward news analysis, I think it could also be read as a piece of Jewish dystopian science fiction.

The final piece, "The Family Romance of American Communism," began as a meditation on the image of the red diaper baby in American life, and my desire for radical roots in my own family tree, in dialogue with Vivian Gornick's 1977 book *The Romance of American Communism*, a long-neglected classic recovered by a younger generation of leftists. The book was reissued, and the essay completed, during the first months of the Covid pandemic, a moment at which—in a strange reversal of the end-of-history consensus—life often seemed to have stalled, while history barreled stupidly along. That spring was the first time I had taken on a serious organizing project, helping my building join the wave of rent strikes across the city and the country in response to the emergency, and the essay ultimately became an attempt to document the way the archive can release political desire and allow it to find expression in political action.

Writing this introduction, I've wished repeatedly for the intensifications and reversals in the news to pause just long enough for me to catch my breath. The idea that history can only be reflected on from a knowing position beyond it is of course a fantasy, and a dangerous one. But for months I held out the hope that some watershed would catalyze the sense of an ending: an election, an inauguration. Then I would know I could stop.

EVER SINCE JOE BIDEN defeated Donald Trump at the polls, political conversations on the left have been haunted by the premise that the upheavals of the past several years, even the storming of the Capitol by white nationalists, were merely decorative, a rococo new look for the same old imperium. Maybe the reignited left itself is a collective hallucination, a coding error singing itself to sleep on the internet each night. Maybe it was all a dream.

The primary fear among leftists consumed by such suspicions, I suspect, is that we ourselves do not exist. If there is in truth no fascist enemy, perhaps there are no real comrades either, and any emergent sense of solidarity today can only promise humiliation down the road. Melancholia itself, Freud said, operated a bit like a dream, a condensed expression of desires consciously imperceptible to a person in its throes. Unaware that something he loves is missing, unable to see his dejection as a form of grief, the melancholic turns on himself as though what he has lost is a piece of himself; he turns on others, too, as though they might be keeping it from him, or he scoffs at the idea that things were ever different. What is it we cannot mourn because we cannot admit we've lost it to begin with?

I keep thinking of a passage from *The Book of Daniel*, a 1971 novel by E. L. Doctorow that comes up briefly in my essay on Gornick. The book's narrator, Daniel Isaacson, is remembering his father, Paul, a character based on the executed Jewish communist Julius Rosenberg. Despite everything he knew about the gross injustice baked into the American project, Paul Isaacson "continued to be astonished, insulted, outraged" that his country "wasn't purer, freer, finer, more ideal," Daniel recalls.

> How much confirmation did he need? Why did he expect so much of a system he knew by definition could never satisfy his standards of justice? A system he was committed to opposing because he had a better one in mind. It's screwy. Lots of them were like that. They were Stalinists, and every instance of Capitalist America fucking up drove them wild. My country! Why aren't you what you claim to be? If they were put on trial, they didn't say, *Of course, what else could we expect?* they said, *You are making a mockery of American justice!* And it

> was more than strategy, it was more than Lenin's advice
> to use the reactionary apparatus to defend yourself, it
> was passion. . . . He would never believe that Amer-
> ica was not the cafeteria at City College; and as often as
> it was proved to him he forgot it.

I don't think I realized I was still melancholically attached to America until Bernie Sanders came along, but then there it was, the ghost of a beleaguered patriotism still fighting after all these years. I wonder, now that I can see it, if I can let it go.

NOW IT IS MARCH, the bitter end of an agitated, microwaved winter. I failed in my attempts to hitch the completion of this introduction to the clamorous demands of the national calendar; one presidency chaotically ended and another listlessly began, dimming the clamor without producing revelation. I was surprised, then, to find myself anxiously pulled toward the arrival of this month, not by the familiar panics of the news cycle but by an undertow of memory. It has been a year since the abrupt end of a short-lived period of hope for US socialists, and the start of Covid's devastation in this country. But the anniversary that seemed to drag me toward it was a personal one, the one-year anniversary of changing my name, an undertaking that seemed impossible until the moment I did it, in a little ceremony at my house on the strange date that arrives only every four years. I have had friends for a long time, but since the veneer of national stability shattered, potential comrades seem to be everywhere, a quiet shift that in some ways has changed everything. It was under these circumstances that I was able to begin transitioning, because I was increasingly able to imagine a world I could live in.

When I changed my name, I felt as though I were sliding into a dark, narrow tunnel. I suppose this sounds like an experience of rebirth, but like the new world struggling to be born, I'm not sure I've emerged: a couple of weeks after the ceremony, quarantine began, a long period of counting the days without knowing what for. It was almost painful to feel the thickening of time, this year, as February drew to a close; I awaited the month's twenty-ninth day, a date that did not come, like the anticipation of a childhood birthday. I shyly allowed myself to mark the occasion, and when I woke up, everything was new again. This episode made me think that even as we struggle to emerge from national time, we should also make new holidays.

—March 18, 2021

April 2016

WHERE THE BOYS ARE

ON BERNIE SANDERS

IN 1960, THE AMERICAN WRITER GLENDON SWARTHOUT, ultimately best known for his novels of the Old West, published a sex farce about a frank, lusty midwestern college girl named Merritt who goes to Fort Lauderdale for spring break to cruise for well-heeled ass. It's March of 1958, and across the Straits of Florida Fidel Castro has called for a general revolt against the Batista regime, but Merritt and her several boyfriends are uninterested. "Most of us had seen stuff about it in the papers," she admits in her frank, lusty way, "but had paid no attention because we were making our own current events." But while getting wasted in a nightclub one evening, they meet a local stripper who happens to be a committed Castroite and tells them of the glories of the Cuban revolution. After hearty debate among the spring breakers about whether their Silent Generation cool will suffer from the performance of too much "embarrassing" political fervor, Ivy League asshole Ryder Smith agrees to join his Big Ten and white-ethnic hipster rivals—and Merritt herself—in an Abraham Lincoln Brigade manqué: the Lauderdale Legion. They immediately crash their borrowed boat. In an epilogue, Merritt is stranded in Florida, knocked up and alone but still plucky, hoping that having her baby will some-how constitute "the spiritual equivalent" of her abortive revolutionary vacation. In 1959, a reporter from *Time* magazine asked a coed why she had come to Fort Lau-derdale for spring break. Her response gave Swarthout the title of his novel: *Where the Boys Are.*

Girls want to be where the boys are, and boys want to be where politics is. That politics is where the girls are is irrelevant in this signifying chain, because girls chasing boys is understood to be *about boys*, but boys chasing girls is understood to be about sex, and therefore, still about boys. "The girls are thinking, 'Where are the boys?'" Gloria Steinem told Bill Maher in February, weighing in on why young women have been throwing their support to Bernie Sanders over Hillary Clinton in their contest for the Democratic presidential nomination. "The boys are with Bernie." Indulging the same semantic slippage Swarthout made more than fifty years earlier, Steinem became a lightning rod in a debate that has circled obsessively around the primaries without speaking its name, about the proper role of feeling—and particularly of erotic desire—in political life. In an unacknowledged way, her gaffe revealed the contours of the terrain on which Clinton and Sanders supporters have clashed from the start. What is at stake is not just gender but *sexual* politics and their tangled legacy in the left-liberal sphere ever since American kids began following their erotic ambitions into the realm of radicalism at the dawn of the Sixties. Sanders, who started college and joined the burgeoning New Left a year after Swarthout's characters hit the beach, represents a specter that has haunted respectable American politics for generations.

For months prior to Steinem's remark (as well as a similarly inapt insinuation from Madeleine Albright the same weekend about "a special place in hell for women who don't help each other"), the dominant meme in the debate over youth, gender, and the Democratic primaries had been the figure of the "Bernie bro," a misogynistic white guy ready for socialist adventure whose anti-Hillary venom confirmed that the left remains an unsafe place for women—a latter-day incarnation, perhaps, of the Lauderdale Legion. The Bernie babe conjured by Steinem—the young woman who campaigns against her own interests, so great is her desire to meet bros—proved such an unconvincing character in the popular imagination that, at least momentarily, the shoe was on the other foot. Clinton supporters were forced to disown what appeared to be a rogue version of the specious and sexist logic that had shored up the construction of the Bernie bro in the first place: the idea that radical politics is, in some inherent sense, a dude sport.

A few days before Steinem rhetorically questioned the location of the boys, and before female Sanders supporters replied resoundingly that they were #NotHereForBoys, I discovered that my gradually waxing enthusiasm for Sanders was in fact about boys. By enthusiasm, I don't mean the fact that I plan to vote for Sanders in the New York primaries. I vote in every local-ass election that comes around, most often in the teeth-gritted way of despondent leftists whose disaffection cannot overcome an addiction to even the charade of democratic process. What I mean is that I was feeling the Bern. *Feelin'* it. Bernie Sanders is a 74-year-old Jewish socialist, one of my favorite categories of person, and a charming, galvanizing specimen thereof. Yet despite my attachment to that person, I live in the 21st century and would love to see the revolutionary energies that have been building through the Occupy and Black Lives Matter movements attach themselves to a candidate fomented in *our* time, attuned to our ways of framing the problems we face. Still, for weeks I felt the Bern coming on. Then, the night of the New Hampshire debate, a friend sent me a picture of Sanders as a young man. His hair is a Dylanesque mop. His glasses could've lost him a midcentury election on egghead grounds. His corduroy jacket is rumpled. He appears to be haranguing someone. He has nice lips. Then I understood.

I wanted more pictures, so I did a Google image search for "young Bernie Sanders." There were pictures of him speaking at a sit-in in 1962, a few dozen kids (mostly white boys, a few girls) cross-legged in a hallway at the University of Chicago. There was one from a Liberty Union Party meeting in Vermont in '71 in which he's distractedly holding his 2-year-old son, sideburns prominently displayed; he's endearingly maternalized by having to perform child care while haranguing. There were a bunch where he got a bit round-cheeked that I sort of skipped over. Then I found the story.

In 1972, Sanders published a piece of writing called "Man—and Woman" in an alternative newspaper called the *Vermont Freeman*. *Mother Jones* dug it up last spring; it's the closest thing Sanders has had to an actual sex scandal, which is to say, not very close. "Man—and Woman" is roughly six hundred words long, and if I had to describe it in genre terms, I would say it is a piece of experimental feminist fiction. Insofar as it has a narrative, it follows its archetypally gendered protagonists, "a man" and "a woman," as their relationship falls apart. It begins, jarringly, with an introduction to both characters' sexual fantasies:

> A man goes home and masturbates his typical fantasy. A woman on her knees, a woman tied up, a woman abused.
>
> A woman enjoys intercourse with her man—as she fantasizes being raped by 3 men simultaneously.
>
> The man and woman get dressed up on Sunday—and go to Church, or maybe to their "revolutionary" political meeting.

Here the narrator breaks the fourth wall and spends several paragraphs engaging the reader in dialogue about the way images of rape eroticize the violence of patriarchy. Things are changing; "women, for their own preservation, are trying to pull themselves together." But the socially enforced "pigness" of men and "slavishness" of women are still locked in a death spiral that destroys them both. Engaging a highly impressionistic version of the anthropological origins of patriarchy (a common starting point at the time for feminist thinkers like Shulamith Firestone and Kate Millett), he writes,

> In the beginning there were strong men who killed the animals and brought home the food—and the dependent women who cooked it. No more! Only the roles remain—waiting to be shaken off. There are no "human" oppressors. Oppressors have lost their humanity. On one hand "slavishness," on the other hand "pigness." Six of one, half dozen of the other. Who wins?

The answer, he concludes, is no one: "Men and women—both are losers." Women's liberation has dredged up paradoxes that neither man nor woman can resolve. "How do you love—without being dependent? How do you be gentle—without being subservient?" Our protagonists' romance turns sour and accusatory.

In the end, "they never again made love together (which they had each liked to do more than anything) or never ever saw each other one more time."

Just as Steinem said, I had followed the trail of boys, and just as she didn't need to say, where the boys are, sexual violence against girls awaits. When *Mother Jones* dug up Sanders's story last May, a brief controversy followed. A group called the Young Conservatives claimed that it was hypocritical for Democrats to criticize Republicans' gender politics in light of "this atrocious Bernie Sanders quote," then presented a screenshot from NBC News. One side of the screen displays the line, "A woman enjoys intercourse with her man—as she fantasizes about being raped by 3 men simultaneously"; the other shows Sanders's face.

But the juxtaposition of text and image made no sense. Huh? Which woman? The syntax alone posed a problem for manufactured outrage. Forget content—we don't expect our candidates to write experimental fiction. Bill Kristol, sensing, perhaps, that the story as such wouldn't scan, used it as an occasion to attack Bill Clinton's wanton sexuality, and, by extension, Hillary Clinton's permissiveness ("Asking several experts for comments on @SenSanders' essay," Kristol tweeted at the other Bill. "Care to comment?") Liberals tried to split the difference. For NPR, to the extent that the piece was "about liberating people from harmful gender norms," it was OK. To the extent that it averred the complexity and violence of desire—Sanders "seems to imply that men fantasize about raping women or that women fantasize about being raped"—it was not. A writer at Slate sensed that something complicated was going on that couldn't be easily unpacked in our contemporary discourse around politics and sexuality; he concluded simply, "The 1970s were a unique time." The controversy died—or seemed to.

Like Sanders's story, Steinem's comment summoned the ghost of debates over sexuality within feminist and left circles that have been largely forgotten, despite having remade radical politics several times over in the 1960s. What we remember instead is the right's appropriation of those debates to its own ends during the culture wars and the ceaseless referendum on the legacy of the Sixties that expressed itself most vividly in the Reagan, Bush *père*, and Clinton years.

In the run-up to the 2008 election, Barack Obama declared the culture wars over. Sensing a weariness with their rhetoric, he deftly cast himself as a fresh face without hang-ups over what he described, in *The Audacity of Hope,* as "the psychodrama of the baby boom generation—a tale rooted in old grudges and revenge plots hatched on a handful of college campuses long ago." As we have seen in subsequent years, this "psychodrama" could not be dismissed so easily as intragenerational squabbling. But Obama's reframing did displace the wars' boomer-centered narrative, and with it, the drama of the Clintons, who served in the right-wing imagination as generals leading the enemy flank.

The last thing Hillary Clinton could have expected in this election cycle, then, was an opponent several years her senior who would take the mantle of the Sixties and start winning young supporters with it. Sanders's "clever strategy of shouting the exact same thing for 40 years," as Holly Wood put it in the *Village Voice*, has hit an unexpected nerve, and with it, reopened wounds that had never really healed to begin with. And so in an uncanny, unspoken twist, the dig long directed at the Clintons from the right—that sexual freedom has turned America into the site of a collective rape fantasy—has been quietly transformed by Hillary's supporters into a line of attack on Sanders. In the *New York Times*, the feminist blogger Jill Filipovic doubled down on Steinem's insinuations, arguing that for the frivolous college girls who support Bernie, "sexism tends to be linked to sex"—a category inclusive of everything from cute outfits to abortion—whereas grown women know that the real fight, Hillary's fight, is about breaking the professional glass ceiling. The poet Eileen Myles, meanwhile, resurrected "Man—and Woman," suggesting midway through a stream-of-consciousness BuzzFeed polemic that Sanders's "love of gang rape" is connected to an intention (details uncited) to defund Planned Parenthood. The rhetoric surrounding Clinton's campaign has become the bearer of a deeply conservative idea that has long posited itself as a progressive one: women can only be safe in the public sphere if sex is kept out.

THE OBVIOUS PROBLEM with Gloria Steinem's boy theory was that it could not abide the idea that young women, thinking for themselves, might for any number of reasons come to different conclusions than Gloria Steinem. Her comment appeared to be an act of erasure: of young women as rational actors, people with commitments along lines of identity other than gender, subjects who might not be boy-oriented at all. There was, however, another way of understanding what she had to say. What if Steinem were simply making a descriptive claim ("this is the situation as I see it"), and we had projected onto it a normative addendum ("and that's terrible")? As Katha Pollitt pointed out in *The Nation*, it's hardly a secret that people make decisions based on "social and psychological factors" all the time. (In an email to Pollitt, Steinem endorsed the reading that she meant Bernie babes no harm.) Since when do we believe in rational actors, anyway?

People who want to upend the social order have always been accused of letting their passions run away with them; acceding to that idea, and even celebrating it, is not necessarily good political strategy. "The fanatic is perpetually incomplete and insecure," wrote the American political theorist Eric Hoffer in 1951, the height of a Red Scare moment in which any expression of political resistance branded its subject as a fanatic. "His passionate attachment is more vital than the quality of the cause to which he is attached." During the same period, American anticommunist crusaders created a panic over the "contagion" of radical politics, intimating that promiscuous social and, especially, sexual behavior posed a grave risk to national security. Accepting the terms of the debate, American communists responded by trying to prove that they were in fact as personally staid, homophobic, and nuclear-family-oriented as the McCarthyist forces

arrayed against them. (Joseph McCarthy and his con-
federates, for their part, could moan and wail and weep
and gnash their teeth as they pleased.)

Thus we return to the finer point that Steinem
put on the question of feelings' relationship to politics.
Not just sentiment, but *sex*, she suggested, was driving
young ladies to a dangerous outpost deep in the wilds
of the public sphere. Whether Steinem was trying to
warn off young female Sanders supporters by invoking
an image of the left as frat house, or teasingly identi-
fying with them, or a little of both, we'll never know.
Either way, she wouldn't be the first.

In *Where the Boys Are: Cuba, Cold War America
and the Making of a New Left*, the historian Van Gosse
takes Glendon Swarthout's novel as illustrative of how
the erotic allure of the Cuban revolution for American youth (largely of the white, male, and collegiate
variety) jump-started the movement of students, civil
rights activists, and antiwar protesters that came to be
known as the New Left. In the 1950s youthful disaffection was widespread but mostly untethered from
organized political struggle. In the 1960s, the New Left
changed that in part by revising the very definition of
the political, taking personal experience—that is to
say, subjective conditions like the state of alienation

produced by advanced industrial society—as its point of departure. "They *had* politics," Todd Gitlin, a leader of the movement, said derisively of the generation of leftists that preceded them. "We *were* politics."

In his autobiography, *Outsider in the House*, Sanders tells a familiar New Left story: upon transferring to the University of Chicago in 1960, he became active in organizations like the Congress of Racial Equality, the Student Peace Union, and the Young People's Socialist League. Shunning schoolwork, he instead (in a likewise familiar boast) studied a self-assigned syllabus of "Jefferson, Lincoln, Fromm, Dewey, Debs, Marx, Engels, Lenin, Trotsky, Freud, and Reich." The admixture of patriotism and Marxism that sutures this list was old-school even in 1960, an inheritance of the alliances forged between American communists and the Democratic party in the 1930s. But the presence of psychoanalysis in the mix, and particularly of Freud's radical descendants Erich Fromm and Wilhelm Reich, is pure New Left. This was the moment of—in Reich's coinage—"sexual revolution."

The "Freudian left" of Fromm, Reich, Herbert Marcuse, and a few others originated in interwar Europe with the idea that the left could only defeat encroaching fascism if it became "the party of eros"

(in the phrase of an American scholar and contemporary of the movement, Richard King). Unlike orthodox
Freudians, who saw the repression of libido as necessary to the upkeep of civilization, the Freudian left
argued that populations forced by moral stricture to
keep sexual energy bottled up expressed that energy
through violence—and that undoing repression would
create the opposite effect. For Reich, writing in Weimar
Berlin, this literally meant that at the level of organizing, communists could bring in the youth being lost to
the aesthetic temptations of Nazism by creating spaces
where boys and girls could mingle. He was rewarded
for these insights by being kicked out of both the Communist parties of various countries and the International Psychoanalytic Association. But once it made its
way to the United States during and after World War II
as part of a wealth of European critical theory, the idea
of sexual liberation—now imagined as an antidote to
the soul-crushing American grind—became integral
to the making of the New Left.

The sexual revolution of the Sixties unleashed vast
quantities of libidinal energy and produced great stores
of ecstatic, politically inspiring feeling—for men. Radical feminism erupted in the late Sixties in large part
out of the fury of women in the New Left whose labor

provided the foundation for that movement but who were constantly marginalized within it. A key critique of the women's liberation movement lodged at what the feminist leader Robin Morgan called the "counterfeit male-dominated Left" was that "the so-called Sexual Revolution" had simply created a new vector of male control. "In addition to suffering sexual frustration from the inhibitions instilled by repressive parents, fear of pregnancy, and men's sexual judgments and exploitative behavior," Ellen Willis recalled later, "we had to swallow the same men's humiliating complaints about how neurotic, frigid, and unliberated we were." Yet this critique of ersatz sexual liberation often morphed into a wholesale rejection of women's sexuality or certain expressions of it, both gay and straight. A critique of *that* critique insisted that sexual liberation needed not to be liberated from its abusers. "What's a party without men?" asked Shulamith Firestone (presumably after taking a long drag on her cigarette) when New York Radical Women, a group she had founded, proposed a gender-segregated soiree. Firestone was no defender of either men or compulsory heterosexuality. But by reframing radical politics as where the *girls* were, sex with boys could be imagined back into the scene on different terms.

As the women's liberation movement splintered in the 1970s, a hard break with the left (which Morgan came to call the "boys' movement") and a dramatic turn toward gender essentialism were often allied in a project by many feminists to redefine the movement as a quasi-nationalistic advancement of "women's culture." Radical feminism had been a largely white and middle-class movement, but also one deeply engaged, if not always successfully, with questions of race and class. Cultural feminists—who often took as their mouthpiece Steinem's *Ms.* magazine—tended to argue, by contrast, that racism and class oppression would wither away on their own if the violent, masculine world order was replaced with the nurturing, maternal values supposedly natural to women. This was not a part of the movement that had space for the messiness of sexual fantasy, including women's. In the Eighties, when "antisex" feminists like Andrea Dworkin and Catherine MacKinnon aligned with Reagan affiliates in proposing legislation against pornography, the link between the rejection of the left and of sexual deviance became painfully clear. Here was a total renunciation of Sixties radicalism in the guise of protecting women from rape. The assumption among some feminists "that sexual coercion is a more important problem for women than sexual repression," which in its most pronounced form relied on "a neo-Victorian view of women's nature," Willis wrote, thus ironically provided fodder for a distinctly anti-feminist idea promulgated by Reagan's New Right: women would be safe from male aggression only in a return to hearth and home.

And then came Clinton.

"I FEEL YOUR PAIN," Bill Clinton told an AIDS activist in 1992, a year before "Don't Ask, Don't Tell" and four years before the Defense of Marriage Act. Clinton himself defended the sanctity of marriage by having tons of extramarital sex with women who mostly, when questioned, avowed consent, but sometimes didn't. While it's true that the most powerful man in the world surely had some leeway to stop rape charges from going anywhere, the same man had an almost equally powerful coalition of Republicans arrayed against him. They produced a 445-page document condemning his sexual exploits, and the worst thing they could come up with was that a cigar is sometimes not just a cigar. Thinking through Clinton is not, as the theorist Fred Moten observed in the aftermath of Monicagate, "a top of the head project." Moten continued,

> Though actually existing American democracy is
> 99 percent whack, there is a coup going on; he's a lech-
> erous harasser but it is obviously important and weird
> to have an openly sexual president; he's a racist and a
> sexist who has butchered black and poor and female
> people, but he doesn't seem personally to hate or, at
> least, be sickened, by the presence of black people or
> women, by the idea of their having, within the whack
> American paradigm, influence and power.

In a perfect inversion of the liberal punditocracy's claim
that Clinton was personally unpalatable but politically
responsible, Moten and the other writers assembled in
the collection *Our Monica, Ourselves*—feminist and
queer theory's most comprehensive response to the
Lewinsky affair—express dismay with the President's
neoliberal policies but identify with and take pleasure
in his eroticization. In permutations of Toni Morri-
son's famous characterization of Clinton as our first
Black President, he appears here—"feminized by . . .
his weight problems, his teariness, his physical affec-
tion, his interest in feelings, his linkage of intellectual
power and emotional bravado," as the contributor Toby
Miller put it—as queer, as woman, as Black woman, as
Jew. The majority of American voters who had elected

him and kept his approval ratings up even during the darkest days of the impeachment hearings seemed to feel similarly. "'[O]rdinary' Americans," Willis points out in her contribution to the volume, "clearly do not share the Washington elite's investment in the idea of the President as moral exemplar, charged with validating the existing structure of (patriarchal) authority"; on the contrary, they had elected him as "a member of the '60s generation, an embodiment of youth and eroticism." What was infuriating was that *this* was the embodiment we were stuck with.

Sometimes in the extended Clinton era it seemed like not just the President, but all the middle-aged flaccidly liberal white men you could see in the movies (*American Beauty*, *Ghost World*) or read about in a novel (*The Corrections*, most books by Philip Roth), had decided to enshrine the historical memory of the Sixties by having sex with younger women, turning back the clock on everyone at once. But who's to say the women in those scenarios didn't have an erotic investment in that historical reenactment as well? Lewinsky herself, in the face of a sexual culture that refused to recognize women as other than objects and victims, unapologetically insisted at the time that she was a sexual subject who took pleasure in the affair. But then again, how fucked up would it be if the legacy of sexual revolution was so deeply embedded in the Clintonian body that there was no other way to access it? In practice, one supposes, women who slept with Bill had a high likelihood of supporting his policy agenda. In the up-or-down logic of representational politics, was a vote for eros, in the Nineties, also a vote for welfare reform, NAFTA, and the crime bill?

Oh yeah, and what about Hillary?

Despite her current iconic status within Steinem's wing of feminism, Hillary Clinton remains essentially outside the intrafeminist debates sketched above. A bit of an anachronism in her own time, Clinton belongs to a different lineage, more connected, in a way, to the long tradition of women social reformers than to the feminists who emerged in the '60s. In her autobiography, *Living History*—a book in which the f-word is scarcely breathed—Clinton writes that in 1970, a couple of days after National Guard troops shot four student antiwar protesters at Kent State University, she spoke at a convention banquet for the League of Women Voters, an organization founded in 1920 to support the cause of women's suffrage. Two years earlier, by way of contrast, radical feminists had protested Richard Nixon's inauguration by burning their voter registration cards; they were "giving back the vote."

Yet the "sex wars" within feminism and the culture wars that dogged the Clintons in the Nineties are intimately connected via the right's appropriation of feminist rhetoric. Their goal is to end, in one blow, the remaining legacy of sexual liberation and feminism itself.* Today, many of Hillary Clinton's supporters—not just responding to continued attacks from the right, but playing offense with Sanders—are tactfully trying to sever any whiff of a connection between the two. Gloria Steinem's comment broke the rules of the game by explicitly alluding to the presence of women's sexuality in the public sphere. Part of why her remark was so hard to parse—was she endorsing this presence or decrying it or simply stating it as fact?—is that her sexual politics have long been riddled with contradictions. "Gloria Steinem went to bed with Norman Mailer out of kindness twelve years after he stabbed his wife," Juliana Spahr reminds us in a recent poem. In the 1980s, she was photographed nude in her

---

* To take an extreme example of what that looked like on the antisex feminist front, Dworkin wrote a piece, published posthumously by her husband during the Clinton/Obama primaries, accusing Hillary of abetting rape by standing by her husband when he was accused (and later cleared) of sexual assault.

bubble bath for *People* magazine and joined the cru-
sade against pornography.

But mostly, those sorts of ambiguities haven't
risen to the surface. Despite the complex mixtures of
attraction and repulsion that jizzed all over Bill Clinton's presidency, Hillary's supporters have maintained
that political emotion is a straightforward, proper or
improper affair. Feeling, when it supports the right
candidate, is pure, noble, and rational. Correctly disciplined sentiment, in this scenario, is imagined to be
precisely aligned with reason, hence the Clinton campaign's ability to claim a premium on both inspiration
(*the first woman president* . . .) and pragmatism (. . . *will
obviously be the person who can* get things done). When
political feeling comes out for the other guy, however, it
is a reminder that affect has no place in electoral politics at all. In this latter view, political feeling is not just
unfair to women because of the sexist *content* that may
come through in emotionally charged rhetoric, but is
also unjust in its very form because women, forced to
be realists, do *not* deal in the emotional realm. Unlike
her opponent, Hillary "doesn't get to be all wild hair
and yelling," the writer of a viral piece published on the
website Pajiba complained immediately before hitting
caps lock and eschewing lowercase letters for the rest

of her article. Undisciplined passions are idealistic, are unseemly, and are tied to unruly bodies like Sanders's, with his wild head of hair that is an affront to all women and their blow-dryers.

Both of these selectively held views rely on a fantasy that voters—that is, responsible voters, not the kind who fall prey to base desires—navigate a simple, unmediated relationship between what they like and what should be. Thus, judging by the frequency with which the argument is made, one of the best things Clinton supporters have going for them is the notion that Clinton's unexpected challenges are due to a "likeability problem." "I Used to Hate Hillary Clinton. Now I'm Voting for Her," announces the headline of a Slate article by the liberal commentator Michelle Goldberg. Goldberg's politics haven't changed—they were and remain close to those of Sanders, she tells us. What changed between 2008, when she excoriated Clinton's political sins, and today, was that her emotional attachments grew up:

> For a progressive, how you reconcile conflicting truths
> about Clinton depends, to some extent, on how much
> you empathize with her. Supporting Clinton means jus-
> tifying the thousands of concessions she's made to the

> world as it is, rather than as we want it to be. Doing this
> is easier, I think, when you are older, and have made
> more concessions yourself. Indeed, sometimes it feels
> like to defend Clinton is to defend middle age itself,
> with all its attenuated expectations and reminders of
> the uselessness of hindsight.

"This is in *support* of Hillary?" a friend asked. Goldberg's counterintuitive approach to political rhetoric— *We're the party of defeat!*—is in fact the more or less official line of the Clinton campaign. Disciplined by the fetters of middle age, Goldberg narrates her march toward reason as a sentimental journey in which, through a growing identification with Clinton, she comes to like the way concession *feels.*

It's hard to argue with desire, and it's easy to get votes if desire is something you can call up. As Freud put it, the unconscious does not have a word for "no." Erotic fantasy has suffused this election cycle whether it's acknowledged, or even recognized, or not. It's been more explicit on the Republican side of the aisle: Trump reassured us of the largeness of his dick, and if the fan fiction he has inspired is any indication, said dick has not gone unappreciated. Clinton's well of erotic charge has always been deeply triangulated with her great-triangulator husband's, and now that well seems to have run dry. In response, she's trying to dam it up with other kinds of feelings, including the feelings mobilized precisely by our feeling her pain as a woman with waning powers of attraction. The problem with doing so is not that it somehow tarnishes her, but that it rests on a claim that desire itself is tarnishing, which creates a self-unraveling logic—*vote for me because you don't want me, and I promise to attenuate your expectations.*

I Still Love Hillary Clinton. I Still Don't Want to Vote for Her. My own profile in political emotion, all but impossible in the eyes of the Clinton campaign, is not a march toward reason but a deepening of continued convolution. It's not just that I enthusiastically cast my first ballot for Bill Clinton in my second-grade class mock election in 1992, and a sentimental, somewhat campy affinity for both Clintons stuck. It's also that, having hit puberty at exactly the right time to learn everything I know about sex from news coverage of the Starr report, their collective role in my constitution as a sexual subject is second only perhaps to that other pair of baby boomers, who gave birth to me. Hillary's incredible pathos, her depths of ambition, the abuse she has borne, her inability to keep her feelings off her face—all the supposedly unlikeable personal qualities that Hillary-lovers love about Hillary, I love too. I can still summon tears at her Oscar lifetime achievement award–ish montage from the 2008 Democratic National Convention, the one where she talks about writing to NASA to find out how a girl can become a lady astronaut. I could look at her all day, would love to crack open a campaign-trail Bud together (she is supposedly very funny in person), if I were in therapy right now I'm sure it would not take long to confirm that I still want her to fuck me. Yet for all the reasons of policy and ideology that leftists who don't want to vote for Hillary don't want to vote for Hillary, I don't want to vote for her either. I will grant that in its details, this profile may be idiosyncratic. But in its general contours, I don't think what I am saying is unrepresentative so much as, within our current discourse, simply unrepresentable.

It's not, then, that my vote isn't about feelings. Like all desire, my attachments to both Sanders and Clinton are weird and hard to pin down: they're about history and nostalgia and childhood and identifications of all kinds. What makes my attachment to Sanders different is that, in the tautological sense that he's (something like) a socialist, and has the energy of preexisting social movements behind him, my desire for him is also a desire for the transformative energies created by social movements themselves. Whereas one thing my attachment to Clinton is *not* about is a connection to a vision of feminist collectivity, because she doesn't come out of or represent a movement that shares such a vision. Without one, feminists are ultimately alone together.

WHEN WE LOOK AT Bernie Sanders, what do we see? One way Clinton supporters attempted to deflect Steinem's gaffe while holding onto its substance was to argue that Sanders is "cool," denigrating him as a dorm-room poster boy but denying that this has anything to do with sex. Of course, cool has everything to do with sex, in politics as elsewhere: it's the best shorthand we've had for the packaging of erotic charge for electoral consumption since Norman Mailer tagged John F. Kennedy "the Hipster as Presidential Candidate" in 1960. More recently, the label has stuck to Bill Clinton and Barack Obama. Since cool is a deeply racialized term—Mailer infamously identified the hipster as "white Negro"—there is a complicated relay here between the racial appropriation going on when white candidates try to be cool, and the racialized charge of the accusation that they have succeeded. Given that our Democratic candidates are currently fighting for the support of a Black electorate whose votes they arguably have not earned, a feud about cool leaves no one looking good.

It's true, though: Sanders is cool. But *why* is he cool? Haranguing Jewish socialists have been out for forty-five years. And since Bill Clinton's administration, the deployment of the Sixties in national politics has been a well-established irritant to the generations of voters that have succeeded the baby boomers. Yet suddenly, Vampire Weekend is performing "This Land is Your Land" at Sanders fundraisers with the candidate on backup vocals. I think what's happening is that Sanders—a New Leftist *older* than the boomers—is in the process of detaching the historical memory of the Sixties from the Clintonian narrative of what happened to Sixties people after the Sixties. A persistent discourse that peaked in the Nineties and waved the flag of boomerdom cynically maintained that only two options existed, or could exist, for aging radicals: sell out, or fade into Lebowskian obscurity. Attempts have been made to fit Sanders into both of these story lines—to tar him either as a tool of the establishment (*he's been in Washington for twenty-five years*) or a dropout from society (*he's only a senator from* Vermont—*hardly a state, more like a toy*). But like the

state of Vermont, the lives that many Sixties movement veterans have made for themselves in regions
at the hazy borders of power and resistance, and the
institutions they have built there are, in fact, real. The
appearance of someone so unreformed on the national
stage has been, I think, a surprising pleasure for many
young people — and conversely perhaps, as Bryan
Williams argued in *The New Republic*, an unwelcome
threat to Hillary's boomer bloc.

Bill Clinton was a dense, voluptuous representa-
tive of the Sixties who held out the promise of accessing that time by accessing his body. Sanders is spindly
and seems, for a politician, unusually self-sufficient;
one meme this year delighted in a video that caught
him dashing spryly through a crowded DC subway
station to make the train. But as the Occupy and Black
Lives Matter movements negotiate their own continued survival, what he offers is something like a grim
but seductively existential promise: the struggle will be
hard and lonely, but if you don't give up, you, too, will
stay cool. It's as though this particular varietal of hip
had been hanging out offstage, forgotten yet exerting
a genealogical pull, then suddenly reemerged Rip Van
Winkle–like, aged and yet strikingly intact. Perhaps
cool hangs around the aging body like an afterimage,

creating a charisma that picks up where more direct forms of sex appeal leave off.

In this sense, the erotics of the Sanders campaign are about nostalgia: a new generation of kids is falling in love with a promise held out by a past one. The problem with nostalgia and the melancholy crushes it begets is how quickly you forget that the snapshot you hold of the time before you were born can't, by definition, include you. When I look at old pictures of young Bernie Sanders, I want to go back and be where those boys were. But I am mindful of the feminists who fled the New Left in droves at the close of the 1960s to start their own movement, who caution me—in yet another historical reverie—it was never for you. And so we have looped around to the start of our tale.

What, ultimately, is the legacy of the New Left in relation to feminism? I've read and thought about this question for a long time, and I still don't quite know how to answer it in the abstract. But it is precisely at this impasse that Sanders's brief and bungled career as an experimental writer gives me hope. "Man—and Woman" is a document of what change within a social movement looks like. It is messy, cocky, timid, flailing, and, read without recourse to historical context, almost illegible. If you try to score it on a spreadsheet of correct political opinion, as internet opinion-mongering is wont to do, it will yield an unsatisfying prime number nowhere near 0 or 100. It is not an unheralded classic of second-wave feminist thought. (Women "are trying to pull themselves together"?) Yet on an account that I think is vital to a sexually liberatory feminist analysis—people including women have sexual desires that can't be cleansed of a relationship to power, but that doesn't have to preclude the formation of gratifying relationships, while what *does* destroy relationships is the real-life violence of patriarchy—he gets it exactly right.

Regardless of the feelings Sanders is stirring up in this election cycle, the limits to the conversation we can have about political emotions have thus far been prescribed by the Clinton campaign. Within those limits, a story about a rape fantasy never stood a chance. I sent the story to the friend who sent me the picture of young Bernie Sanders. "Mainstream politics is a series of magic words being repeated like a ritual incantation— 'free trade,' 'values,' 'security,'" he wrote back. "'Rape' is outside that political vocabulary. It cannot even be contextualized." The same goes, I think, for *fantasy*, and this was precisely the argument of the Freudian left and its New Left and feminist inheritors.

Fantasy permeates this election cycle as it permeates all national life, but it cannot be actively affirmed in public speech, and this is precisely the point at which utopian thought—say, the mere *contemplation* of socialist revolution—is arrested. At a moment in American history when the rhetoric of fascism blares perhaps more loudly than ever before, it might be time to let it in.

MISSING TIME

ON *THE X-FILES*

S. WAS THE ONE WHO USUALLY WROTE OUR FANFIC. IT'S ALL there in my files, packed into the box my mom sends me from the Valley when I decide to write about the show. It tends to be in screenplay form and leans toward the carnivalesque. It's 1970s night at the Haunted Mansion and we are all together: Mulder and Scully, me and S.; their nemesis the Cigarette Smoking Man, a deep-state puppeteer responsible for countless acts of terror, and our nemesis Ms. Simonds, an English teacher at Gaspar de Portola Middle School whose crimes I cannot recall. Exene Cervenka of the legendary LA punk band X makes a cameo appearance. After a few tequila-and-opiums, our gang throws open the gold-plated doors at a members-only club hidden in

Disneyland's New Orleans Square and discovers we've passed through a portal to the Life Café, where everyone hangs out in *RENT.* We order soy dogs and sing.

My stuff sounds stilted and self-conscious by comparison. My one real contribution to the genre was a naive first attempt, a fanfic that could not yet speak its name, which appears as a notebook entry from the beginning of seventh grade.

9/22/97
Dear B.,

God, we have a lot of catching up to do. Well, first of all, between now and maybe a month ago or so, I became an obsessive *X-Files* fan. Call it hanging out with S. too much, but it is seriously the best show ever made. I even have a completely screwed up, totally bogus theory about it. This is it:

The X-Files is not a Fox 11 TV show as commonly thought by a vast majority of sane people in the world. It is instead written and produced by the secret government. Now, Marissa, you may ask, what the hell are you talking about? Well, according to my theory, this Secret Government began around the time of World War II. What they intended was to gradually build suspicion about their existence until people began rebelling. Then they could declare the rebels, who would be the majority of the American people, a threat to society, and have them vaporized. (Am I starting to sound just a wee bit like a militia member here?) Unfortunately for them, the cold war and McCarthyist policies and stuff started. So people got their attention off the Secret Government, and vented their anger at the Russians instead. OK, skip to the '80s. The cold war is almost over, and the SG (you figure it out) guys are thinking, OK, now we can get down to business. So they create fictitious people like George Bush and Bill Clinton to lure the people into a false sense of security. But all the while, they're dropping hints to get people neurotic. So there should be a surge of UFO sightings soon (which, of course, are just planted by the SG) and that's how *The X-Files* started!!!!! Don't you just love my logic?!?

Anyway. I started the coolest club. It's called the Messed Up People Club.

Things continue in this vein.

Sixth grade had not gone well. Around the beginning of the school year, I had become an ardent communist. I knew about communism from musicals and Jewish historical fiction and the night of the big earthquake when I was 8, when everyone left their houses at four in the morning to loop past the palms on March Avenue in silent procession because the location of safety had moved outside. A few months later, a big tacky house that appeared to have only cracked in a few places went on sale nearby, in the foothills at the far edge of the Valley, and we moved in. My mom spoke glowingly of our proximity to nature. Rabbits ate the lawn, and sometimes coyotes ate the rabbits. My parents hired a gardener to replace the grass with Astroturf. It was the mid-1990s, but like a lot of people, we lived outside historical time.

As for the ardency, who can say? Like everything I started wanting in the months before my first period, the desire for communism seemed both endogenous and alien, secret and self-evident. To me it seemed to explain a lot of things, but I tried to keep quiet about it because it was, as we said at the time, very random. I found a Marxist reader in the den among my father's college books; it was too hard for me, but I buried it like a fetish under my bed. It had always been my custom to hide the media that could hurt me, like novels with bees or Nazis, around the house. The philosopher Ernst Bloch distinguished between two currents of Marxism, one warm and one cold. The cold current—"the detective glance at history"—was about where capitalism came from, how it worked, and ways it could be overthrown, and about all this I knew very little. My current was the warm one, all strikes and hammers and bread and roses, a child's communism. Sometimes, if I started having too much fun being with other people, I laughed so hard I peed in my pants, and a warm current froze into a cold one down my legs.

People think that only adults felt groggy and homesick after the end of history, but children were sad, too. In the Valley, you could dress up as any decade. Kids were covered in meaning. Or, I thought we were. Obviously I was bullied. Every day after school I sat at my desk drawing automated rows of smiling girls and tried to divine who would eat whom, just from looking. My only friends, B. and the other fuzzy glowworms who lived in my stomach, formed a council to address the crisis but schismed. At the end of the school year, I addressed them sternly in my notebook.

6/5/97
A Letter to B.:

I am writing this because I don't think you should be a
communist any more. In that Marxist book or whatever

it is that Daddy has it says that the main idea in communism is to abolish private property. Well, obviously, that has to do with economics and all that. I think when we grow up we should focus on something less extreme and something that will actually be paid attention to by regular people. Here's a list of practical causes and stuff that I can protest/advocate at some point in time:

Fur
Abortion
Gun control
Death penalty
Drugs (but not heavy ones)
Assisted suicide

love,
marissa

The following entry, from August, concerns a birthday party to which I was not invited. By September there was S., and *The X-Files.*

SOMETHING HAD HAPPENED, and we could not remember what it was. In *Missing Time,* a 1981 best seller that helped establish the conventions of the alien abduction memoir, ufologist Budd Hopkins explained that evidence of an extraterrestrial visitation often took the form of precisely this sort of mysterious gap in experience. Abduction was a way of describing rupture in its purest form, a literal wrinkle in time. I could relate: it wasn't like I had a better excuse for being such an old-fashioned girl. But I was not alone. In the 1990s, anyone could be abducted, though the aliens seemed to have a thing for white girls, and a way of making men feel like white girls even though they weren't. Weird syndromes coagulated everywhere. The deeper in the suburbs they appeared, the more mysterious they seemed, like signs from another world. A postwar infrastructure of office buildings and tract homes designed to cordon off the white middle class from the contagious city turned out to be built from noxious materials that made people sick. Asbestos, formaldehyde, and 4-phenylcyclohexene, or "new carpet smell," dewed up in moldy corners beneath the level of perception. Veterans returning from Iraq reported a rash of problems—memory loss, respiratory trouble—that they attributed to chemical exposure. When no physical marker could be found for Gulf War syndrome, mass psychogenic illness, a new term for hysteria, was extended for the first time to men.*

The X-Files was born into this biosphere in 1993 on Fox, an upstart network trying to figure out how to undercut its more established rivals with niche programming like *The Simpsons* (1989 to present) and the Fox News Channel (1996 to the end of the world). A seriously ambitious program, *The X-Files* "made TV cinematic," as the critic Theresa Geller put it in a recent monograph, inspiring waves of cerebral genre programming and launching the careers of showrunners like Vince Gilligan (*Breaking Bad*) and Frank Spotnitz (*The Man in the High Castle*). But the show was also a quasi-respectable cousin of *Jerry Springer* at a time when reality, too, was remaking TV. In this sense the series wasn't science fictional at all, but took place in a world just like our own, where women being poisoned by their microwaves floated around with Lyndon LaRouche supporters and AIDS denialists and 12-year-old ex-communists in dubious pursuit of a history of the present. There they were, serially archived on a single flashing screen, from the

---

* See Michelle Murphy, *Sick Building Syndrome and the Problem of Uncertainty: Environmental Politics, Technoscience, and Women Workers* (Durham: Duke University Press, 2006), 3, 81, 93.

Loch Ness monster and the chupacabra to the JFK assassination and the defamation of Anita Hill. In the last years of the 20th century, this solar system of conspiratorial thinking was where the postmodern condition lived its best life. You could find yourself in cozy exile there, social theorists said, if you'd tried too hard to picture technoscientific global capitalism and your brain broke. I'd barely begun to try, and mine already had.

On *The X-Files*, the United States government was a shell company for extraterrestrial interests in our GDP of biopolitical slop: neurons and wombs, oil fields and cornfields, radio towers and internet cables, Nazis and bees. The cold war wasn't really over, but it had also never really begun, the whole thing having been, as Thomas Pynchon put it in *Gravity's Rainbow* twenty years earlier, a front for the war of multinational technology cartels against everyone else. Now, in the Nineties, world-historical conflict farted in its fresh grave as hoax and scandal filled the deregulated airwaves. Cable news proved such a deadly carrier of "subliminal messages" that in one episode, people in a DC suburb watch TV pundits weigh in on Bosnia and are hypnotized into homicidal rage against their loved ones. In other words, paranormal activity caused by

US–alien collusion manifested on a day-to-day basis as unaccountable violent symptoms bugging out the collective sensorium. In the parlance of the show, this sort of thing was an X-file, a local mystery with national implications that the federal government didn't *want* to solve. Such cases fell to an odd couple of FBI agents: Fox Mulder (doofy, irreproachable David Duchovny), a believer bent on avenging a government cover-up of his sister's abduction, and Dana Scully (acute, deadpan Gillian Anderson), a medically trained skeptic assigned to spy on him. Mulder and Scully spend the series investigating strange phenomena, from a 120-year-old serial killer who hibernates between meals of human liver to an American luxury liner perpetually invaded by Germans because it's always 1939 in the Bermuda Triangle, on behalf of a regime that wants to snort their brains. *The X-Files* may not have been the best postmodern novel ever written, but it was, despite stiff competition, perhaps the longest.

The show ran until a few months after September 11, 2001. It spawned two forgettable feature films and started up again as a series in 2016 in a painful nostalgia exercise; this spring, it was ostensibly laid to rest for good. *The X-Files*'s creator, Chris Carter—a SoCal boy who spent thirteen years at *Surfing Magazine* before he started the show—shot episodes like small movies where the sublime architecture of conspiracy in the post-Watergate thriller entered the orbit of Lynchian Americana: *All the President's Men Meet the Log Lady.* Some episodes layered one aesthetic atop the other: in countless scenes, girls in white nightgowns run barefoot through the woods illuminated by the glare of spacecraft or SWAT teams. Others seemed located halfway in between, in endless gray suburbs where Washington and Main Street alike flicker in between commercials on a half-watched screen before a working mom is gobbled up by a swarm of irradiated cockroaches. Either way, everything looks like Vancouver, where the show was shot through its fifth season, creating the uncanny impression that, in the Nineties, the entire country was a Northwestern logging town haunted by industry. The show's devotees created an online subculture largely populated by female X-philes, who debated the relationship between its conspiracy-driven "mythology" arc and its less sweeping but often more satisfying "Monster of the Week" one-offs, as well as the persistent question of whether Mulder and Scully should bang. ("Shippers" said yes, "no-romos" said it would ruin the show.) At a time when being obsessed with stuff on the internet was

still the province of freaks and geeks, the show's pro-
ducers winked back, turning losers into collaborators.

Teetering between police procedural and science
fiction, *The X-Files*, Geller notes, forgoes the positiv-
istic comforts of a regular forensic drama, in which
truth can be discovered and justice served in the space
of a single episode. The show's collision of genres, she
writes, conscripts Mulder and Scully into the role of
social detective—Fredric Jameson's term for a sleuth,
sometimes a policeman or a journalist, but sometimes
a Jane Q. Public or even a whole community—who,
motivated by forces beyond the need to file a report,
approaches "society as a whole" as "the mystery to be
solved." As such, our heroes stumble through each
X-file in a state of epistemological crisis. Halfway
through the pilot episode, driving one stormy night
down a back road in an Oregon town zapped with
extraterrestrial enterprise, the agents are enveloped
by a halo of light, and their car goes dead. When the
light subsides, Mulder checks his watch and squeals
that nine minutes have vanished into thin air. "Time
can't just disappear!" Scully, panicked for the first time,
stammers through the rain at her giddy partner. "It's a
universal invariant!" Mulder, riveted beyond gloating,
pants back, "Not in this zip code."

By granting impressive measures of scientific reasoning to one and gestalt interpretation to the other, the show gives its leads a basic measure of dramatic and intellectual equality. Neither agent is Sherlock to the other's Watson, and each contends with the harassment that befalls women who do autopsies and men who read tea leaves. Both are smart, stubborn, lonely, and brave. At the same time, a persistent sleight of hand gives *ontological* priority to Mulder: it's his world we're visiting, and in the final instance, his research methods tend to be the ones that work. (Not coincidentally, Anderson is a serious, thoughtful actress who would go on to play Lily Bart and Nora Helmer. Duchovny, at his best, just kind of *is* Fox Mulder. Had he not dropped out of Yale to play gender-bending roles in *Twin Peaks* and porny indie films, he might have finished his dissertation on Pynchon and his peers, "Magic and Technology in Contemporary Fiction and Poetry.")

To be Scully—or, in a more archetypal sense, to be "a Scully"—is to insist on the laws of physics even as the aliens stretch you out on board their ship. It's to begin a sentence, as she does in "Die Hand Die Verletzt" (The One Where Devil Worshippers Run the School Board), "I mean, there's nothing odd about—"

only to be cut off by toads falling from the sky. It's to climb the rungs of an institution that seeks to push you off the ladder, to stoically salute your authoritarian father's coffin, to relax by studying the DSM-IV on a Friday night over a glass of wine, and still to somehow find yourself among mutants, the odd girl in a different boys' club than the one you'd intended to join. As with her predecessor Clarice Starling, Jodie Foster's dogged young criminologist in *The Silence of the Lambs*, Scully dares to look into the hearts of the coldest killers, and they alone dare to look back.

To be a Mulder, on the other hand, means your ears buzz with white noise but your sacred duty is to keep it Real. Because you're obsessed with getting outside, you take a job way on the inside, put on the gray suit you were born in, and work both for and against the (Cigarette Smoking) Man, who considers vaping you every eighth episode but then just maims you again like a favorite broken toy. Your basement office under the panopticon is so close to where the maps are made, it's off the map. You're a polonium-tipped dart's throw from knowledge but so far from power that they don't even bother harassing you half the time. So you curl up in the belly of your own surveillance, eat sunflower seeds out of the bag, and jerk off at your desk beneath your iconic poster of a grainy UFO with its block-lettered caption, I WANT TO BELIEVE. "It's interesting," a shape-shifting rapist tells him in an episode called "Small Potatoes" (The One Where Mulder Gets Impersonated by a Man with a Tail). "I was born a loser. But you're one by choice." To be a Mulder is to be a kind of idiot, and to be right. In many episodes, he crumples to the ground as though literally stricken by the force of terrible knowledge. I did that too, I bragged to my journal. And I liked to watch.

IN OUR BOOK, even in the late section titled "The Great List of Differences," S. and I never quite come out and say that she is a Scully and I a Mulder. This might appear in retrospect like a correction for the show's own bias, a critique of how contemporary metaphysics still estranges science from magic after all these years, or a mature recognition that Mulder and Scully aren't *real*. In fact, I think S. was happy to acknowledge her own allegiance to the latter, while I was too uneasy to admit to such a fundamental split.

I had known S. since the second grade. We liked each other because we were both serious, but for the same reason didn't play together much. Once I borrowed an armload of her books, then forgot about them for so long that we had outgrown them by the time I brought them back. In middle school we became part of the same carpool, and at the start of seventh grade she became what, had we been paranormal investigators, I would have called my partner. It was 1997. Earlier that year, the thirty-eight remaining members of Heaven's Gate, a UFO cult that started in the '70s, washed down phenobarbital with vodka for the same reason everyone did what we did in those days: the millennium was coming.

My mom, a special-ed teacher, diagnosed me with autism spectrum disorders only when I was getting on her nerves, which in those days I usually was. S. presented her with a complicated case. At school, most kids on the spectrum had trouble getting along, or only hung out with each other. S. gravitated in their direction, but she was as cool as an algorithm, or a brand, and could sense the same quality in the objects around us as disinterestedly as a nurse checking for fever. Later, when there were more of us, we spent years trying to account for her unaccountability, as though she had joined us from another planet. In retrospect, though, she was simply from a feminist cyberpunk future that never quite happened. She was a tiny child, pale with freckles and acne, who wore a spiked dog collar and soft bright T-shirts from babyhood and who seemed to have more processing power available to her than anyone anyone had ever met. She learned programming languages and, like the girls who took Korean lessons after school, turned her handwriting into a font. At one point she tried to make pocket protectors happen and almost succeeded; if we'd had more internet in those days, she might have. She was mean to boys and they fell in love with her; if we'd had more internet in those days, she might have become one herself. When she wrote about middle school as an adult, her alter ego was a secret robot.

To her great frustration, S. had to share a small room with her sister, but in my mind her house was, if not a portal to the Life Café, at least a peephole. Through it could be glimpsed a full-spectrum pastiche of cultural politics: her aunts and uncles on one side included Marxist art historians and a regional leader of the Objectivist society; on the other, a Sonic Youth producer with a bathtub full of records. It was her father, who drank wine and watched baseball and read John Barth, who informed me one day in our carpool, "Work is hell." S. and I silently agreed that I would come as close as possible to taking on her tastes, habits, and Myers-Briggs classification (INTP: the Logician) and use the results to establish our superiority to the normies around us. Throughout my files from this time, our belief in the typological power of codes we had made up ourselves appears with a conspiracist's selective rigor. ("I've finally figured out why my mom and I don't get along," I wrote. "She's an ESFP!") In the notebooks I manically maintained in the fall of seventh grade, I claimed that we had become so close, we seemed to be merging into one.

I kept, for those months, not one but two journals. In my regular journal, I fantasized about making a suicide pact with a boy in a Pearl Jam shirt, and global annihilation as an antidote to slow violence. I copied S. I complained about my mom, who compared me during one fight, I reported indignantly, to another young woman lacking in "fundamental values": Squeaky Fromme, the Manson girl who'd plotted murder from Spahn Ranch just a few miles up the canyon from our house. In my *X-Files* journal, which opens with an apology for "my ever-insistent urges to write even *more* rambling pages" about the show, I traced David Duchovny's face out of *Us Weekly*, hit critical walls (what was the proper level of detail to include in an episode recap for which I was the only reader?), and tried to suck a political education out of my television.

HISTORY, WE WERE TOLD in the 1990s, was something that happened to other people. The recent past was littered with code-named police actions that, rendered pointless by the evaporation of the cold war, no longer even had the dignity of the unmentionable. Conservatives kept building monuments to the death of communism that no one wanted to visit. Liberals wanted to forget the whole messy business and gave themselves endless Oscars for movies about World War II. Only fools with sheaves of xeroxed newsletters thought they were smart enough to construct a narrative out of a deafening drone. The more distant past, upon inspection, turned out to be much the same, leading some to suspect that history had never happened at all. There were, however, exceptions to the rule: events taken to be unique in their world-shattering horror, and exceptional people who had come near them and gotten away no longer quite themselves. We, too, could be exceptional: if we were good and listened hard, history could become something that happened, though only by proxy, to us. Every year on the Day of Remembrance, survivors came to Hebrew school and asked us to feel on our skin the licks of the Shoah's eternal flame and to guard with our lives its redemption in the birth of a handsome nation. In history class in regular school, we learned nothing at all. And yet the past kept ghosting through like reruns.

Reruns were the form in which I watched the show, already five seasons in and beginning its long decline by the time I got on board. Seeing its baffling conspiracy arc unfold out of order saved me the hassle of getting fully invested in a plot that often made no sense. True to its times, *The X-Files* lacked a show bible, the reference guide typically used to maintain consistency over the course of a series. Yet even at its most labyrinthine the program imparted the crucial thesis that cataclysmic violence was not merely the stuff of historical memory, but an ongoing process of natural history still ravaging lands and bodies zoned for continuous extraction. "Something just clicked about the whole Holocaust," I wrote, shaken, after watching season two's searing "Anasazi" trilogy (The Ones Where Mulder Gets Decolonized), in which we learn that the Kissinger-era State Department collaborated with ex-Nazi scientists on the production of human-alien hybrids, using tribal populations as test subjects. When Mulder finds evidence, the government destroys

the tape, but Navajo code talkers have already memo-
rized its contents. The Final Solution, the episodes suggested, emerged not from the depths of an unfathom-
able hell but had a *logic* that preceded the camps and
survived their dismantling; maybe it was even right at
home in the United States. Here, if memory stood a
chance at enduring through the body, it was lodged in
throats intubated by colonial force.

Did I get all that, or did it go over my head entirely?
Was it even there to begin with? *The X-Files*, a show
whose social detectives are at the end of the day still
cops, occupied a cunningly ambiguous slot in the ideological lineup of its equivocating era: symptomology
without diagnosis, conspiracy without collectivity,
paranoia for its own sake, a bossa nova accelerationism
for a rainy evening with an eclectic drug collection and
nowhere to go all night. Critics spanning the political
spectrum loved it, especially those concentrated at its
weirdo ends like S.'s aunts and uncles. The appeal to
academics on the left of a series about intrepid hauntol-
ogists trapped in an institutional maze run by evil
overlords perhaps goes without saying. The show was
like Duchovny: if it hadn't landed on Fox, it would have
just taught cultural studies. Many of its most poignant,
sophisticated episodes are seminars on the power, and

the limits, of Mulder's methods for patiently sifting through piles of cultural detritus on the lookout for connections between dubious Monsters of the Week and tortuous conspiracy arcs. On the dust jacket of her excellent cultural history of ufology, *Aliens in America: Conspiracy Cultures from Outerspace to Cyberspace*, the Marxist political theorist Jodi Dean broke the fourth wall of scholarly detachment entirely, posing in front of an I WANT TO BELIEVE poster and appearing to suppress a giggle. But the libertarian right boasted hardcore fans as well, and for similar reasons. The show represented resistance to neoliberal governmentality in the form of clandestine cells: hacker collectives, militias, cults practicing archaic magics bright and dark. In doing so, it seemed to beckon its own cult following, wrote the libertarian scholar Paul Cantor, who has devoted hundreds of admiring pages to *The X-Files*, "as if the program were trying to replicate in its audience what it shows in the world at large."

For me, too, *The X-Files* held out the promise of subculture, the meaning of style. I studied Mulder's methods—suspend disbelief when doing fieldwork, wink at your interview subjects—and tried to make them my own. But because I was 12 and had never heard of anything, the show functioned even more literally as a dictionary of esoteric knowledge from which America could be inferred. The secrets made me giddy and desperate, like hearing an incredible bit of gossip over a wiretap. S. and I got on the phone every Sunday night after the show ended and talked for hours.

Fandom was a way of organizing knowledge and desire, a kind of epidemiology. You learned from the cluster of objects that drew near you what kind of person you were. The internet was like that, too: it sorted. S. loved it there and from it brought back news of our cult. From her I learned of the epic online battles between shippers and no-romos, and S. and I took up the cause of the latter with the passion of hardheaded agents who thought romance was for little girls. Around the beginning of seventh grade, men from the phone company had come to my house, too, and installed our own beeping, flashing modem. My journal makes no mention of the internet's installation, but by the end of the year, it's there in every entry, a thrilling, ugly hassle. I went through the motions of fury with my parents for limiting my access to its catacombs, but even S. knew I basically agreed with them: I wanted it to leave us, and hoped it still might.

Sometimes, through the entropy of perversion, curiosity, a hunch, I found myself in bad company. "I

finally managed to subscribe to the INTJ page, and
they're all Ayn Rand freaks!" I griped to my journal.
"'Mercy is a trait that only an F can possess'!" And yet
my diary itself, in the moments it draws most clearly
from my *X-Files* notebook, sounds unnervingly like
the adolescent fascism of 4chan. There is a short story
about the Pentagon "vaporizing" rebels in Montana, a
state my mother often used to illustrate the point that
even in the Nineties, a Jew could not go everywhere.
There is a poem called "Awaken" in which the speaker
steps into reality, "where bureaucrats are not cheerful
pink bunnies / And dreamers do not rule the world."
It wasn't that I'd switched sides in my private political
pantomime, where communists and fascists were still
at war. If anything, I probably rested too easy in the
assumption that I never could. It was simply that my
enemies, who filled the web with paeans to the intellectual superiority of white men who liked to code, had
the advantage of actually existing. I dabbled in their
language because, as far as I knew, I did not.

On New Year's Day, I described a fight with my
parents in which I lost access to language and became
"a dead circuit." Chunks of the recent past had gone
missing, and the cloud of absence threatened the borders of the present. The visitors had landed, Jodi Dean

wrote that year: the internet was changing people; it had gotten into our blood, scrambling codes. Just as Budd Hopkins, the ufologist, had promised, we were no longer the watchers but the ones being watched. I still have information sickness. I don't know what it's really called.

On January 2, though, I had better news. I took out what amounted to full-page ads in both my regular and *X-Files* journals, indicating in giant purple letters that something had changed in my house, something that meant I would now be able to watch the show every night:

WE
GOT
FX!!!

And then, for months, I barely wrote at all.

WHEN MY JOURNAL picks up again around the start of eighth grade, a new kid has emerged, kind of hyper, in the midst of a determined cultural discovery process. I loved Sylvia Plath and the Violent Femmes and "anarchists" and my JNCOs. My mapping had become more focused; there were fewer global conspiracies and more genealogies of punk. An *X-Files* soundtrack had introduced me to Nick Cave, and a Nick Cave CD had a cover of "All Tomorrow's Parties," and "All Tomorrow's Parties" led me down the stairs to the Velvet Underground. At some point in the process I no longer needed the show: I could read lots of things now. It was 1998. In Calabasas, where the rich girls from Hebrew school lived behind locked gates, a new outdoor mall was built in the shape of a fake Umbrian plaza. They called it the Commons.

BY THE TIME S. AND I graduated from middle school, we had built a world together. *M. and S.'s Book*, made one long weekend after graduation in the summer of 1999, catalogued that world before it was destroyed, as we knew it would be, by our departure for different high schools: a math-and-science magnet for her, a humanities one for me. Like an eponymous first album, it did not have another name. Its cover is adorned with cutouts and stickers—a Lisa Frank palm tree, Beck, the Ayatollah Khomeini, a potato. Its handwritten pages are filled with song lyrics and comics and fanfic and assessments of our friends and endless inventories of our universe.

> Things We Want (in S.'s writing), No. 41: No tongue so I can sound like the Sex Pistols (M. thought of this first).

Stuff That Scares Us (S. again), No. 31: Obsessive fans-turned-assassins. Where the hell is your brain, I'm talking to you, Mark David Chapman.

Things That Depress Me (my writing), No. 14: How Columbine made all these shitty laws happen and now you can't wear trench coats and stuff.

____ No. 15: How my dad fucked my computer and I can't get in.

____ No. 16: How communism didn't work.

We wanted to distribute our book widely, but my mom read it, noted that it was, among other things, a burn book—"Oh, and her choreography sucks," S. wrote of one friend—and forbade this, instead driving us to Staples to print the only two copies in existence. "It's just me and S. again," I wrote in my journal at the end of that summer, "and god we had the most depressing conversation tonight. About how we're so worried about *everything*: high school, college, life. How this era totally sucks and even our parents admit they had it easy, but at the same time we are so lame cuz all our music is old and we act like it came out yesterday. We are obsessed with old dead people. Everyone is fuckin dead or they own stores in places like Silver Lake." On bad days, I admitted, "I completely lose myself in time."

MULDER AND SCULLY'S partnership could not survive the turn of the millennium and neither could mine and S.'s. In the show's final seasons, the agents finally seem to be sleeping together, ruining an important source of dramatic tension exactly as we knew it would. Both leads had pulled back from the series and were partially replaced by generic opposite-gendered investigators. George W. Bush was elected, the twin towers fell, and the national appetite for conspiratorial fantasy was sated, for a while, by the nightly news.

By that time I had stopped watching. S. stuck with the original series until the end; I quit when the going got tough. She wanted to remain an extraordinary child and I was trying to become a more ordinary miserable teenager. Neither of us could keep up with the other, and we suffered and quarreled. For S., computing offered safe passage to wonder; the beauty of form was on the inside. I remained locked out; computers break when I come near. At Armenian church camp one summer, she welcomed Jesus into her heart and kept him there for a few years, and I discovered my own bewilderment in the face of belief. She was celibate; I just couldn't get laid. We both loved other girls but not quite, we decided, each other. Later, she would study engineering, and I would study its critiques. Later still, she would move to the Pacific Northwest, build brains for a big company, and fill a mansion with marvelous toys and then children to play with them. I moved across the country to my city, where I wander around staring uncomprehendingly at objects and waiting for them to stare back. I still have my I WANT TO BELIEVE poster over my desk. It was the first thing I ever bought online.

What is easier to see with greater distance is that the epistemological tension that had held the show together—the coy flirtation between magic and science—had been consummated, just like the relationship between Mulder and Scully or between conspiratorial fantasy and political reality. We had been literalized into a strange new lifeworld entirely saturated by computer technology. *The X-Files* filled its characters with alien-manufactured microchips, but it never really caught up to a world with smartphones. Detective work on *The X-Files* had happened under the cover of darkness, the agents' flashlights casting single beams across a blackened screen. But by the turn of the millennium, the night was fading. In Russia, a space company made plans to dot the sky with satellites that would reflect sunshine back to earth at all hours, creating "daylight all night long."* The satellites never launched, but it didn't matter. The new order of things had eliminated shadows, and with them, an entire methodology for seeing in the dark.

The *X-Files* reboot first aired in the early months of 2016, when the air was humid with denial. Fittingly, the real problem is the lighting. Anderson has a self-help book out; Duchovny, back from rehab for sex addiction, wrote a novel in which farm animals representing Israel and Palestine make friends, and has a Twitter account for his dog. In the new episodes, they uncannily seemed to be playing themselves—her with sharpened cheekbones, him with an open top button on a crisp white shirt—like they'd just come from brunch in Santa Monica. But an influx of daylight created a problem for the series on another level, too. In "My Struggle" and its sequels (The Ones That Felt Longer Than a Knausgaard Novel), the show's updated myth arc revolves around our protagonists' attempt to deal with a strange new bedfellow, a popular right-wing

---

* See Jonathan Crary, *24/7: Late Capitalism and the Ends of Sleep* (New York: Verso, 2014) 4.

conspiracy peddler on the model of Alex Jones, who is both clearly odious and possibly onto something. For all the original program's storied self-reflexivity, the new show could not figure out how to live up to its twist, both jaw-dropping and enragingly inevitable, on the old one: *Fox Mulder Meets Fox News.* The call is coming, all too obviously, from inside the house.

The reboot rebooted again in early 2018, its problems further magnified by everything we've learned in the past two years. Season eleven, does, however, include one all-time great episode, "The Lost Art of Forehead Sweat" (The One Where an Alien Does a Trump Monologue), a bittersweet film essay on the impossibility of *The X-Files* in a "postconspiracy" age when power refuses to go through the motions of concealing its most brutal machinations. In one montage that spans the Reagan through Obama years, a nebbishy paper pusher evolves from a bored postal clerk to a napping Securities and Exchange Commission operative to a CIA agent casually waterboarding a bound man to a drone operator accidentally bombing a far-off wedding, all from the comfort of the same cubicle. At the episode's end, Mulder and Scully meet a bedazzled extraterrestrial ambassador who has arrived in a flying saucer to inform them that the aliens' study of Earth is complete; the intergalactic confederation no longer wants anything to do with us. "We are building a wall," he intones cordially but firmly. As a parting gesture, he gives Mulder a trim, leather-bound book called *All the Answers*, "in case you have any questions remaining."

"It's OK, Mulder," Scully reassures her stunned partner when the spaceship has whizzed off. "There will always be more X-files." "No! It's not true!" Mulder howls, hurling the book and crumpling to the ground.

The *New York Times* recently reported that the Pentagon has spent millions of dollars on UFO research in the past decade. Weird objects are appearing in the sky again, or maybe they're just Teslas. It's all been met with a collective shrug.

As usual, Mulder was right.

IN THE MONTHS BEFORE the election, I lost my method, too. I was trying to write my own dissertation about magic and technology in contemporary literature, and left my city to be alone with my devices. Keeping myself safe from stories and refusing to stumble on mysteries, my information sickness spread until I could not know things at all. A dead circuit. Instead of a map, Trump's giant face.

That November, the earth opened and we fell through the cracks, picking up speed. It wasn't one big hole but endless small ones, like gas coming up through the tundra, or like our house in the Valley with its network of hidden fissures that opened up one day twenty years after the earthquake. Broken clocks floated by. They were melted but no longer missing. I am a communist again, like lots of kids. As I write this, children across the country are marching out of their schools together because the location of safety has moved outside. The rich are planning missions to the stars.

The world felt strange in the late 20th century when politics congealed into fandom, like being haunted by ghosts. Now that fandom on the right has melted back into politics, it feels psychotic, like being stalked by monsters or chased by cartoon frogs. When we get accustomed to the political unconscious becoming conscious, the imperceptible perceptible, we say we are woke; the Nazis say red-pilled. It is uncanny to remember a time when we spoke only through the things we liked and wore, like looking back at cultists who think they have outgrown the swaddling of history, but in fact simply will not speak the names of their devils and gods. When alt-right thinkers complain about a specter they call postmodernism, I wonder if they miss it.

It's hard to say whether the new show we are living in is a sequel to the old one, or just its reboot. We were in the park at night, a different friend and I, a different time. I'd tangled myself in a swing and was spinning round and round when he told me about Roko's basilisk. The basilisk, born on an internet chat forum for the philosophical wing of the new tide of fascism, is a super-powerful artificial intelligence from the future. He wants you, earthling, to work toward his establishment as a supreme being ruling a neofeudal order. He will not bug you if you do not know his name, but once you do, you're in or you're out, and if you're out he will fuck you up, even if he has to rebuild your consciousness out of machine dust in order to do it. The basilisk is a folktale of our time. In him, we meet the ultimate conspirator in the shape of a chintzy Monster of the Week. Like a bit of malware in your head, he insists his story be passed on.

"Let him come," I said to my friend. "If we refuse to speak of him, we give him the power of our childhood phantasms. The enemy has revealed himself. Now we can fight."

"You are a white girl in the park on acid," he said. "On the border, they are building camps."

I put my foot out sharply and stopped spinning. One looks at one's friends and neighbors and wonders who will turn. One turns to oneself.

I do not know if we can organize from a place this disorganized. But I want to believe.

April 2019

THE DOUBLE'S
ALLEGIANCE

ON PHILIP ROTH

MIDWAY THROUGH PHILIP ROTH'S BRILLIANT AND
maddening 1993 novel *Operation Shylock*, Roth's alter
ego—who this time around is simply named Philip
Roth—takes a road trip from Jerusalem to Ramallah
with a long-lost friend, a Palestinian intellectual named
George Ziad. All the way there, past innumerable
checkpoints, Ziad rants about the corrosive psychic
effects of Israeli apartheid—on Jews. In Ziad's view,
hegemonic support for the Zionist project has rendered
the Jewish people tragically "goylike." He wonders
whether they can snap out of it. "What *happens*," Ziad
demands, "when American Jews discover that they have
been duped, that they have constructed an allegiance

to Israel on the basis of irrational guilt, of vengeful fantasies, above all, *above all*, based on the most naive delusions about the moral identity of the state?" Philip doesn't answer. The friends arrive at their destination, the military tribunal of a Palestinian teenager accused of throwing Molotov cocktails at Israeli soldiers. Israeli army personnel have injected the boy with drugs to prevent him from speaking at his own trial.

A furor erupted last month when Ilhan Omar, a freshman congresswoman from Minnesota, described the obstacles she has faced as an outspoken Muslim supporter of Palestinian liberation. Omar observed that support for Israel—like loyalty to the gun or fossil fuel industries—remains entrenched in American political life thanks to the efforts of a powerful lobby. "I want to talk about the political influence in this country that says it is OK for people to push for allegiance to a foreign country," Omar said. Never mind that supporters of the Israeli government often speak of a "special relationship" between Israel and the United States. Omar's opponents seized on the word *allegiance*, claiming that it could only signify one thing: anti-Semitism. Democratic lawmakers responded treacherously, proposing a resolution against anti-Semitism designed to censure their colleague.

But the smear campaign against Omar did not go as planned. Young Jewish leftists disagreed with its premise forcefully enough that their response, along with resistance from within the legislature led by the Congressional Black and Progressive Caucuses, forced party leaders to retreat. As though intent on playing out a twist from a Philip Roth novel in the writer's memory—Roth died last year at the age of 85—Democrats amended their resolution at the last minute to condemn hate itself.

When the rising generation of unapologetically anti-Zionist Jews looks for its ancestors, will they remember Roth for asking the question: *now* what happens? Or will they remember his silence in the face of it?

I READ *OPERATION SHYLOCK*, an unhinged entry in the Roth canon poised at the juncture of his midcareer metafiction and his historically sweeping late work, several months after his death, and for an admittedly vulgar reason: I wanted to know if, with regard to the moral identity of the Jewish state, we were on the same furious team. I already knew that Roth was important to me. As a teenager, I first read *Portnoy's Complaint* (1969), a stand-up special in the shape of a novel in which, over the course of a single therapy session, a young man recounts a life so bloated with "shame and shame and shame and shame" that he suspects he's stuck "in the middle of a Jewish joke." I remember being glued to it in the car on the way to the religious school I attended for four hours after regular school every Tuesday and another four hours on Sunday mornings, which I hated but did not realize I could quit. Later, my favorite Roth novel was *The Ghost Writer* (1979), a work in which Anne Frank may or may not be alive, hot, and living in the Berkshires. In that book, a short story by Roth's alter ego Nathan Zuckerman skewering Jewish life in his hometown earns him a stern letter from Judge Leopold Wapter, one of the most prominent Jews in all Newark, complete with a numbered list of leading questions:

> 1. If you had been living in Nazi Germany in the thirties, would you have written such a story? . . .

> 6. What set of aesthetic values makes you think that the cheap is more valid than the noble and the slimy is more truthful than the sublime? . . .

> 8. Can you explain why in your story, in which a rabbi appears, there is nowhere the grandeur of oratory with

which Stephen S. Wise and Abba Hillel Silver and Zvi
Masliansky have stirred and touched their audiences?

All these questions capture the easily wounded pride
barely concealed behind discount mandarinism char-
acteristic of postwar American Jewish respectability
politics. But the one about Stephen S. Wise, an early
20th-century Reform rabbi who lent his name to a large
synagogue in Los Angeles that we didn't go to, still
makes me blush harder than any joke about jerking off
into chopped liver. Respectability can be doubly shame-
ful because its banality hardly seems worth the dese-
cration. Roth showed me my life was worth profaning.

Allegiance to Israel was an intrinsic element of a
stretch of American Jewish life that encompassed both
the aspirational midcentury milieu Roth frequently
took on, and the comfortable suburbs I grew up in
at the century's end. Ilhan Omar was talking about
military aid, but I am talking about summer camp,
where once, in a forced-choice game, we were asked,
"If America and Israel went to war, whose side would
you fight on?" (I assume we were meant to draw the
conclusion that America and Israel must never go to
war.) Many of us were brought up to believe that our
real home lay in a country where only Jews belonged.

But the increasingly confident anti-Zionist Jewish left in the United States has rejected the idea that our lives are given meaning by the bloody realities of Jewish settlement on the colonial frontier. We are diasporists: we believe we make our homes through solidarity with the stateless wherever we are.

I wondered if Roth might be one of us. The author mostly wrote about Jews in America, but Israel hovers around the edges of many of his novels. *Portnoy's Complaint*, for instance, ends with Alexander Portnoy visiting the holy land. He finds it difficult to take the place seriously. "In their short pants," Alex muses, "the men remind me of the head counselors at the Jewish summer camps I worked at during college vacations—only this isn't summer camp, either. It's home!" The sheer ubiquity of Jews in the country reminds him of a familiar racial hierarchy, too: "Hey, here *we're* the WASPs!" In the end, Alex finds that—in a punchline to the joke that is his life—he is unable to get an erection in the Jewish state. "Where other Jews flourish," he proclaims, "I now expire!" In Roth's 1986 novel *The Counterlife*, meanwhile, Nathan Zuckerman flies to Israel to confront his philandering brother, who has abandoned his family in Newark to become a West Bank settler.

Roth was typically more of an aesthetic than a political radical even in his youth, and the grand old manhood that graced his last decades marked a progression, not a break. But I suspected that, beyond the pleasures of endlessly refracted representation, he also offered a resource for Jewish anti-Zionism hidden in plain sight. And so Roth died and, bored of the lionizing obits about the prince of American Jewish letters, I decided to read *Operation Shylock*, which I knew concerned a Philip Roth impersonator peddling a political program called diasporism. As it turned out, *Operation Shylock* had seen me coming a mile away.

OPERATION SHYLOCK is about a writer, Philip Roth, who discovers that a huckster calling himself "Philip Roth" is on the loose in Israel, using the writer's brand to raise money for his own cause. Fake Roth, whose true origins are shrouded in mystery, has been traveling the world proclaiming Israel "the gravest threat to Jewish survival since the end of World War Two." Well, fair enough. But Fake Roth believes, further, that Jews should return en masse from Israel to eastern Europe, and has met with Lech Walesa, who led Poland's Solidarity movement, to discuss their repatriation—a dubious notion, not least because many Jews do not descend from eastern Europe to begin with. More dubious still is Fake Roth's reasoning: "horrendous as Hitler was," he argues, the Third Reich was only a flash in the pan—whereas the hatred of Arabs for Jews is intractable, cosmic, racial. The impostor's sought-after allies include Meir Kahane, the real-life leader of the Jewish Defense League, a militant Jewish supremacist organization that birthed a far-right Israeli political party now caucusing with Benjamin Netanyahu's Likud party in the Knesset. Zionism's ultimate mistake, Fake Roth concludes, is that, by settling in the Middle East, Jews have reneged on fulfilling "the great Jewish European destiny." (Oh.) Upon learning all this, Real Roth flies to Jerusalem to confront his doppelgänger. Considerable hijinks ensue.

The trap was set and I fell in. I had wanted Roth—the real real Roth—to articulate a diasporist politics for me, and the very premise of *Operation Shylock* suggested that he felt this demand and scoffed at it. For the first few chapters of the book, I was impressed by his devilishness in forcing me into company with a character for whom "diasporism" is simply the name of a rebranded white supremacy. But I was also disappointed. Fake Roth is a stunted schmendrick; Real Roth—let's call him Philip from now on to

keep ourselves sane—nicknames him "Moishe Pipik,"
Yiddish for "Moses Bellybutton." It seemed to me
that there was something stunted, too, about Roth's
take on diasporism, an epic troll standing in for real
thought. But then George Ziad showed up—with his
own never-mentioned double, Edward Said, hovering
behind him.

Ziad, a beloved graduate school classmate of Philip's who long ago gave up a professorship in the United
States and moved home to Palestine, quickly comes
to occupy the heart of the novel. Out of touch for
decades, the men encounter each other by chance (or
is it?) in the Jerusalem shuk and warmly reunite. Ziad
is brilliant and inconsolable regarding the fate of his
people under Israeli rule. And, even in the terms given
to us by *Operation Shylock*, he is a diasporist.

In the remarkable scene in which Philip and Ziad
drive to Ramallah, Ziad, who has confused Philip with
his pretender, declares himself to his companion as a
devoted follower. In one sense, Ziad's support for the
odious Moishe Pipik is strategic, even diplomatic: he
desires the end of Jewish sovereignty in his homeland,
and Pipik's debased diasporism promises a path toward
this end. Yet he also shares with Pipik—and, it seems,
with Philip and with Roth—a conviction that for Jews,

the creation of Israel has meant the tragic loss of diaspora itself. In Palestinian history, the year 1948 marks
the Nakba, or catastrophe, in which Zionist militants
razed hundreds of villages, massacring their inhabitants and creating nearly a million refugees. In Israeli
history, it marks the birth of an independent state. But
Ziad claims to speak from the perspective of Jewish
history; in his telling, 1948 becomes a kind of Nakba
of the Jewish soul, the outcome of an "unthinkable
interrelationship, bordering on complicity" between
Nazis and Zionists who shared the dream of wiping
out the cultural, social, intellectual, and political life
of diaspora Jewry and all it stood for: ambivalence,
absurdism, emasculation.

For Ziad, diasporic Jewishness survived the birth
of Israel only as a phantom. American Jews, racked
with survivors' guilt in the wake of the Holocaust,
pinned their sense of peoplehood to an identification
with "a Jewish military state gloating and triumphant"
and dedicated themselves to justifying the continued
expansion of that state by consecrating a lost sense of
victimhood. Other than that, they had pretty much
assimilated. "Green lawns, white Jews—you wrote
about it," Ziad tells Philip. "You crystallized it in your
first book." Ziad's impassioned postcolonial reading

of Philip's oeuvre—which is, of course, identical to
Roth's—finally descends into fawning desperation.
"Philip, *you are a Jewish prophet and you always have
been*," he concludes. "How can I serve you?"

At the end of *Operation Shylock*, Philip is abducted
by the Mossad and asked to become a spy for the Jewish state. His handler takes a dark view of his own
work. "I am a ruthless man working in a ruthless job
for a ruthless country," Agent Smilesburger tells his
captive. But at least, Smilesburger adds pointedly, he's
not trying to wheedle out of the charge by performing
political agonies. Philip takes the job, which leads to
Ziad's death and ultimately to the bowdlerization of
the very novel we are reading. At the request of his
handler, Philip tells us, he has excised a chapter about
his mission, the titular Operation Shylock. We know
only that he has infiltrated a PLO meeting in Athens in
order to obtain intelligence about "Jewish anti-Zionist
elements threatening the security of Israel."

I came to *Operation Shylock* hoping it would
offer evidence toward an anti-Zionist interpretation
of Roth's work; Roth laughed, wrote the exegesis himself, and fed it into the shredder. Within the world
of the novel, Pipik's epic trolling and Ziad's strong
reading are inextricable: the latter draws its strength

from the slapstick and yet deeply serious misunderstanding enabled by the former. Ziad radicalizes Roth's own hysterical vision of postwar American Jewishness, drawing out of it a language with which to resist Israeli occupation. Pipik's diasporism is a doppelgänger of this critique—a straw man, a fetish, an idol for Roth to break. Pipik reveals that behind every refusal of ethnonationalism lies another ethnonationalism. This is, of course, a fascist lie. But by presenting diasporism as a seduction that Philip resists, Roth can reframe his alter ego's quietism as negation. For all its surreal trappings, the novel slides into what C. Wright Mills called "crackpot realism," an ideological mode in which complicity with power is recast as the refusal of illusion. As the critic Moustafa Bayoumi observes, this mode would become central to "the late aesthetics of the War on Terror" in thrillers like *Homeland* and *Zero Dark Thirty*, in which tough-minded American government agents discover that there is no alternative to the torture of Muslim enemies. We might recall here that Philip Roth is a favorite novelist of Barack Obama.

FOR MUCH OF HIS CAREER, Roth's muse was his own status as a pariah in the American Jewish community.

Roth's detractors, especially after *Portnoy's Complaint*, ran the gamut from local rabbis to intellectual leaders like Irving Howe and Gershom Scholem. In many of his novels, these critics were repurposed as interlocutors. "If you had been living in Nazi Germany in the thirties," they ask him, "would you have written such a story?" This maneuver puts the meta in Roth's metafiction. It compels us to understand literary self-consciousness not as a trick but as a record, one side of a writer's long-running spat with the world.

This approach to gathering literary material also required Roth to exaggerate the terms of his excommunication. The scandalized reviews and pulpit denunciations he received were real—but so were the Jewish book prizes he began winning in 1959 with *Goodbye, Columbus*, and wrote about much less often. In *Operation Shylock*, he calls his own bluff: at one point, Pipik smirks that Philip is "coming back into the Jewish fold again because he wants a Nobel Prize." Roth's stature, even or especially in the establishment precincts of American Jewish life, only increased in the decades that followed *Operation Shylock*, as the writer turned his hand to national epics like *American Pastoral* (1997) and *The Plot Against America* (2004).

But even Roth's most outré work has been kosher ever since the old politics of respectability gave way, in the Jewish world as elsewhere in American life, to the cynical co-option of dissent. This reclamation has occasionally bordered on the grotesque. Shortly after the arrest of Harvey Weinstein on sexual assault charges, a hot take in the Jewish web magazine *Tablet* used *Portnoy's Complaint* to justify describing Weinstein, almost fondly, as "a deeply Jewish kind of pervert." The article's author, the religion journalist Mark Oppenheimer, noted that Portnoy lusted after all-American white girls; Weinstein, likewise, assaulted many non-Jewish women. Oppenheimer argued that Weinstein's sexual pursuits, like Portnoy's, signified an anxious celebration of Jewish entry into the promised land of whiteness—although Oppenheimer used the deracinated term "power," the better to continue the celebration. It was a reading worthy of Moishe Pipik, and the magazine was forced to apologize.

Green lawns, white Jews. A triumphant march toward empire, with some hang-ups mixed in. It would be a great loss if Roth were remembered as an exponent of this vision for American Jewry rather than its sharpest satirist—if he were buried, essentially, in one of his own traps. At the same time, I don't think we can look to him as a diasporist forebear. This is not, in the end, because I suspect Roth of more than a grudging allegiance to Israel. It is, rather, because his allegiance to America ran so deep. Throughout Roth's work, not Israel but the United States is a Jewish haven that must be safeguarded. In *Operation Shylock*, Philip sacrifices Ziad not because he hates Palestinians but because, when his adventure is over, he can go home. We might look instead to the real Edward Said, who could not. For good reason, Said sometimes described himself as "the last Jew."

Late last month, Israel began bombing Gaza again. Donald Trump recognized Israel's illegal occupation of the Golan Heights, while at the AIPAC conference in Washington DC, Netanyahu lashed out at Ilhan Omar as Democrats stood by. We are allowed to speak about this now—*some* of us, sometimes. I remember when the silence was louder, when bombs fell on Gaza in 2008, and the rambunctious newsroom at the *Jewish Daily Forward*, the newspaper where I worked as a reporter, grew quiet and withdrawn. I remember accompanying a Birthright Israel trip sponsored by *Tablet*, where I worked a little later, laughingly assured by my editor that I could staff the trip *and* write the exposé. I remember how much time I spent imagining I was a spy, then discovering I was just a patsy.

It is a relief to have blown our cover. But we should be wary of the special dispensation to speak, as the lost children of Zionists, as others continue to be silenced. I am looking forward to the return of the Jews, and watchful already for false prophets of diasporism.

THE RIGHT KIND OF CONTINUITY

ON JEFFREY EPSTEIN

WITH NOAH KULWIN

REAL-LIFE CONSPIRACIES POSE A CERTAIN CHALLENGE FOR political analysis. Take the case of Jeffrey Epstein, the financier whose indictment in early July has produced revelations shocking even in an age of cartoon villainy. What is there to say about an international pedophilia ring linked to former US presidents and Mitteleuropean aristocrats, which operated for decades with near impunity thanks to the prominence of its participants, at the behest of a billionaire whose private plane was nicknamed the Lolita Express?

It is likewise awkward for Jews when a Jewish public figure so perfectly embodies an anti-Semitic caricature. And here too—even with Woody Allen atop the alphabetical list of associates whose names appear in Epstein's leaked little black book, and Alan Dershowitz allegedly availing himself of Epstein's underage girls even while getting him a sweetheart deal in court—it has been difficult to know quite what to say. After all, Epstein's friends also included plenty of prominent non-Jews (Donald Trump, for instance). But two stories that broke last week have turned the Epstein case into a specifically Jewish debacle—not the generic kind an anti-Semite might dream up, but one rooted in the particular realities of the contemporary US Jewish establishment.

At a glance, these new disclosures have little in common. The first, a story reported by the *Forward*, detailed fallout within the Jewish community over the formerly close ties between Epstein and Leslie Wexner, a lingerie billionaire and a major Jewish philanthropist. The second revealed that—in the deadpan words of the *New York Times*—Epstein had long "hoped to seed the human race with his DNA by impregnating women at his vast New Mexico ranch." Only the former story explicitly dealt with the Jewish world—and yet it was the latter that elicited widespread social media responses like the writer Ayelet Waldman's. "I just keep muttering to myself, 'Oh my god this is so so so so so so so so so bad for the Jews,'" Waldman wrote. "Am I the only one?" (She was not.)

Looking at these stories side by side, we might ask: what can it mean that someone so very bad for the Jews has operated so close to the center of power in the American Jewish community?

OVER THE PAST FEW WEEKS, Wexner—whose retail empire includes Victoria's Secret and Express—has mostly appeared in the news in response to a persistent question: Where did Jeffrey Epstein's money come from? For a man who owns private islands, Epstein's assets appear to be relatively meager. The financier seems to have acquired much of his wealth in the 1990s and early 2000s through the largesse of ultra-rich friends like Wexner; Epstein called Wexner his mentor, and the press has often described him as Epstein's "only known client." In addition to cash, Wexner gave Epstein power of attorney, which allowed him to perform financial transactions in Wexner's name. He also gifted Epstein his Upper East Side manse, then handed over the Boeing 727 that Epstein would turn into his infamous party plane. Though Wexner has not been directly accused of wrongdoing, he appears to have tolerated Epstein's habit of gaining access to Victoria's Secret models by posing as a talent scout for the company. Wexner claims he knew nothing of Epstein's abuses against women until Epstein pleaded guilty to solicitation charges in 2008; at that point, Wexner and his foundation say, they ended the relationship.

Within the Jewish institutional world, however, Wexner's relationship with Epstein is significant in a different way. Wexner is among a small number of Jewish community megadonors, billionaires who provide an outsize and growing proportion of funding for communal organizations and to a large extent determine what those organizations look like. Along with Sheldon Adelson, Charles Bronfman, and a few others, Wexner has spent millions of dollars on institutions ranging from Birthright Israel—which has sent over 500,000 young diaspora Jews on free trips to Israel—to the Jewish Theological Seminary, where Conservative rabbis are ordained. The Wexner Graduate Fellowship, a prestigious and often career-making award, sponsors leadership training and graduate school tuition subsidies for an elite cadre of future rabbis, educators, and other Jewish professionals. Epstein was closely involved with Wexner's charitable giving; together, for instance, the two men helped fund the construction of a new building for Harvard's Hillel. Tax filings suggest that Epstein spent six years as a trustee of the Wexner Foundation, and that the foundation gave millions of dollars to pet projects of his own. (Epstein also donated to Jewish charities himself, though at a comparatively modest level.)

These ties are now stoking anxiety and division behind the scenes at Jewish institutions led by Wexner-affiliated professionals. Last month, the *Forward* reported, a former student at Mechon Hadar—a co-ed egalitarian yeshiva in New York—emailed the school's listserv with a plea for the institution to cut ties with Wexner in light of the unspooling allegations against Epstein. Mechon Hadar's president, a prominent rabbi (and a stepson to former US senator Joe Lieberman), responded by censuring the student, implying that he would be unwelcome in the Hadar community until he performed teshuvah—repentance—for having "called out" the connections between Wexner, Epstein, and the school in a community forum. Wexner-backed institutions may well hope that any outrage currently directed at their benefactor goes the way of allegations against Michael Steinhardt, the Birthright cofounder and megadonor accused last year of serial sexual harassment — which is to say nowhere. Steinhardt remains on Birthright's honorary board; his money will likely continue to be welcome throughout the mainstream Jewish world.

Lacking a broad base of support, Jewish organizations are increasingly dependent on alms from an ever older, richer, and more conservative donor class. In this sense, the likelihood that the Jewish world will continue to harbor high-level sexual assailants is simply a matter of odds: the violence of rich and powerful men against women, as we continue to confirm, is staggeringly commonplace. A community reliant on the generosity of such men is thus particularly vulnerable to their abuse.

On another level, though, the problem is even more circular than these practical considerations would suggest. The donors who rose to power in the Jewish community at the end of the 20th century built their philanthropic vision around the promotion of what came to be called "Jewish continuity." They commissioned extensive surveys of American Jewry and found that the kind of Jews they recognized seemed to be disappearing: synagogue membership and affinity for Israel were in decline, interfaith marriage was up, and Jewish fertility rates were down. In response to this perceived crisis, the Jewish establishment poured millions of dollars into programs intended to reproduce the community "in its own image," as the sociologist Shaul Kelner put it in an article by that name. Reproduction itself, both biological and social, is at the heart of Jewish continuity programming. The demographer Steven M. Cohen, who produced countless statistical reports on the community at the behest of the donor class, liked to put it bluntly: if institutions wanted American Jewish life to continue, they would have to prioritize the goals of "creating more Jewish marriages and filling more Jewish baby carriages."

Feminist critiques of continuity discourse have become increasingly audible within the mainstream Jewish world, intensifying last year after Cohen himself was accused of serial sexual harassment. "How surprised can we be that a man whose entire worldview hinged on women having more babies turned out to have no respect for women when it came to personal sexual boundaries?" the writer Rokhl Kafrissen asked in the *Forward*. In practice, though, Jewish organizations designed to promote a large-scale reproductive project have continued to do just that—and to enable the abuses that come along with it. "We're tantalizing you with 'you will hook up and you will marry,'" a former Birthright staffer told *Jewish Currents* in our investigation of sexual misconduct on the Israel tours. "The trips promote allegiance and a lack of critical thinking. And to talk about rape culture, you have to be able to think critically."

Cut to Epstein's New Mexico ranch, where, according to the *New York Times*, the financier intended to have twenty women at a time inseminated with his sperm. Epstein was interested in transhumanism, a theory of human perfection via technological manipulation that—like its predecessor, eugenics—is shot through with racist and reactionary ideas. Allegedly inspired by a defunct operation to stockpile the sperm of Nobel laureates, Epstein cultivated relationships with Harvard scientists whom he believed could help him in this and other transhumanist endeavors. He hoped to improve the human genome, to cut aid to the poor as a bulwark against overpopulation, and to cryogenically freeze his own brain and (allegedly egg-shaped) penis. Donations to Harvard got Epstein, who did not attend college himself, in the door; he was welcomed as a patron and interlocutor by high-profile researchers even as some, like the neuroscientist Steven Pinker, eventually distanced themselves. Dershowitz, who as a Harvard Law professor regularly attended lunches Epstein hosted for the scientists, told the *Times* he was "appalled" to learn about Epstein's eugenic ambitions, but their friendship continued.

These revelations suggest that Epstein is not only a sexual assailant on a grand scale, but one who believes, on the basis of bloodlines, in the *righteousness* of some version of his sexual politics. Clearly, Harvard—even if it knew nothing of Epstein's predation—should be held accountable for inviting someone promoting these views into a prominent role at a research institution. Is the same true for the Wexner Foundation? No evidence has yet emerged connecting Epstein's eugenic ambitions to his Jewish philanthropic ones. It should concern us that Epstein long had Wexner's ear, but then, we were already concerned.

ALL SCANDALS ASIDE, Jewish establishment donors and leaders obsessed not only with Jewish continuity but the *right kind* of continuity—ardently pro-Israel children of two Jewish parents—have failed on their own terms. Perhaps the most publicly identifiable organization of millennial Jews is IfNotNow, which rages against the moral obstinacy of the establishment. Jews of color, drastically undercounted by establishment

demographers even as they have been instrumental-
ized as Zionists, are demanding recognition. And
Steven M. Cohen's research, with its dire predictions
about American Jews intermarrying into extinction,
has been called into question for its narrow definition
of Jewishness. The language of continuity "told people
who fall outside of the parameters set primarily by men
that their ways of being Jewish are not valued or valu-
able," as three Jewish women professors—Kate Rosen-
blatt, Lila Corwin Berman, and Ronit Stahl—wrote in
a *Forward* op-ed last year.

   These are consequences of the Jewish establishment's tacit bargain with billionaire donors, which
realigned Jewish institutions with a set of priorities
never agreed upon by the wider community. This
bargain created a communal leadership disconnected
from many of the Jews it claims to represent, and prox-
imate to figures like Epstein.

   Rather than endlessly tracing these webs of
influence, we might do better to listen for ideological
echoes. With his insemination plan, Epstein conjured
a eugenicist fantasy a Nazi could love—and one that,
in the context of his proximity to Jewish philanthropy,
also feels like a crude parody of Jewish summer camp
seen from the perspective of a megadonor. Of course,

his plan was nakedly about his own mass reproduction, while the Jewish philanthropic establishment aims to reproduce an entire community. But the establishment has projected its own face onto that community, refusing to recognize deviations that would disturb this image—including the deviation posed by women's reproductive autonomy. Which is the greater narcissism?

June 2020

THE FAMILY ROMANCE OF AMERICAN COMMUNISM

ON VIVIAN GORNICK

WE HAD JUST LEFT THE NEW TRADER JOE'S ON GRAND Street, and I was pointing out the old Lower East Side settlement house, when my father remembered the note he'd made to tell me about the communist neighbors. He played at their house all the time, he said, until his mother stopped speaking to the communist mother because she had called him an intellectual snob. We all shrugged, like, fair enough. He'd been a piano prodigy, precious and arrogant.

"How did you know they were communists?" I asked. "I guess they must have talked about it," he said.

We walked up the front steps of Hillman, the complex in the Grand Street co-ops where my parents stay when they visit me in New York. The communist parents never got married, he added, "because the party said marriage was a bourgeois institution, or something." I said the Communist Party was actually very pro-marriage at the time. Both my parents stiffened a little, as if I were splitting hairs. "Well, for whatever reason, they never got married."

The Grand Street apartment belonged to a distant relative on my mother's side, an elderly Orthodox woman I didn't know. She had lived an hour away in Queens for decades, but could neither bring herself to sell the property nor set foot in it, so her daughter loaned it out to visitors. It comprised two units that had at some point been merged into one, folding out from the center like an accordion. There were two front doors, though only one was in use, and two kitchens, one for milk and one for meat. The rooms were filled with archaic media: video recordings of sitcoms and Holocaust documentaries, almanacs of baseball statistics and Billboard charts. That afternoon I began interviewing my parents at the plastic-shrouded dining table that sat before a large mirror in one of the apartment's two living rooms. I was trying to piece together a political history of my family. Sometimes I worried that I didn't have the right genes to be a leftist.

We all thought the apartment was a total trip and enjoyed the sensation of being trapped there. Few of our ancestors had spent meaningful time in New York before heading west to the Canadian prairies or Southern California. These cousins, on the other hand, had owned an umbrella shop on Orchard Street, lending a ring of authenticity to the crap lying around the apartment—rabbi figurines just shy of anti-Semitic caricature, yellowed sheet music—that differentiated it from identical junk back home. But there was also something arrestingly strange about a home abandoned in this way instead of aging along with its inhabitants; every anachronism seemed art-directed, carefully selected to capture the gestalt of the whole, like a movie set or a house museum. It was an honor to be related to such canonical people.

NEW YORK'S 20TH-CENTURY high-rises are black boxes, concealing class differences behind a uniformity of ugliness. There are private developments and low-income projects run by the city and middle-income co-ops run by the state and complexes built by unions as worker housing and complexes built by socialist organizations for their members. Some high-rises, like the Grand Street co-ops, used to be public and are now private. Those that have remained public, holdovers from another time, have waiting lists that can stretch over decades, so the easiest way to get an affordable unit is to inherit one. Communists' apartments were all alike, which is to say, they looked like everyone else's.

Throughout much of the world, Communist Party membership skewed heavily male. In the United States, however—where the party had accumulated around seventy-five thousand members at its peak in the 1930s and 1940s, as well as many fellow travelers—it was largely composed of families. In immigrant enclaves, communism gave foreign-born parents and their American-born offspring a common language, reproduced through a network of Sunday schools, youth groups, and summer camps. McCarthyism tore many communist families apart, but only strengthened domestic ties in others: ejected from the public sphere, party life was pushed more deeply into the private one.

For anticommunists, the notion that families could incubate radical politics rather than buffer against them belonged to the world of horror movies. Communists were *Twilight Zone* people, body snatchers, homosexuals, Jews, a charade of averageness. At the same time, their ease at blending in suggested that the American spirit had already been snuffed out, by television or the monotony of office life. You never knew if the Kremlin was involved in these endeavors. Strong mothers were necessary to the protection of the free world, but threatened to smother the same masculine autonomy they were charged with cultivating. Any overbearing matriarch could be Angela Lansbury in *The Manchurian Candidate*, a communist spy trained in mind control who uses playing cards to bewitch her war hero son into becoming an assassin. Any spineless son could turn out to be a red diaper baby.

Julius and Ethel Rosenberg, perhaps the most famous American communists, lived with their two sons a few blocks from Hillman in a middle-income housing development called Knickerbocker Village, also notable for the rent strike that took place there during the Depression. The Rosenberg trial was, as the novelist William Gass put it later, "a family affair." Ethel's brother, David, and his wife testified against his sister. (He would ultimately recant, saying he had done it to save his own family.) Ethel's mother was furious that she had involved David in communist organizing and did not attend her daughter's funeral. Half the ensemble was Jewish: the judge, lawyers on both sides.

Jewish anticommunists trying their best to assim-
ilate into white America found the entire thing humiliating. For the critic Leslie Fiedler, Knickerbocker Village
was a "melancholy block of identical dwelling units
that seem the visible manifestation of the Stalinized
petty-bourgeois mind: rigid, conventional, hopelessly
self-righteous." Fiedler hated Ethel's solicitous letters
to President Eisenhower asking him to take pity on her
"small unoffending Jewish family" and vowing that she
"would be homesick anywhere in the world" for the
USA. He hated the memory of the 1930s, when Jews
became spokesmen "for that sentimental radicalism
which best reflected the Depression mood of the United
States." Without elaborating, Fiedler darkly reminisced:
"What a strange marriage we celebrated then, without
quite knowing it, between Karl Marx and the Jewish
Mother." Almost as though he were ashamed of where
he came from.

Sometimes my mother accuses me of trying to
replace her, and it's true that I have imagined subbing
out my parents for people who look just like them but are
completely different. Freud calls this fantasy the family
romance; he says it happens a lot. There was a conspiracy of resemblance outside my window: the LA suburbs
played every city on television, even New York. Once, at

10 or 11 years old, I was home alone making cookies and I crossed our wide, empty street to ask a neighbor for an egg, like a housewife in a sitcom. I was reprimanded; the neighbors would think I was neglected. What could be more awful than a child with a nice single-family home wanting to live in an apartment?

VIVIAN GORNICK'S MOTHER, Bess, believed that the Lower East Side was for "Jewish gangsters" and that "politically enlightened" Jews, communists like herself and her family, belonged in the Bronx. The borough was home to the city's largest socialist housing development, the United Workers Cooperative Colony, built by Jewish radicals and known simply as the Co-ops, but Gornick, born in 1935, grew up in a tenement apartment—"a building full of women," she writes in her 1987 memoir, *Fierce Attachments*, locked together in poverty and sexual frustration. Caustic and resourceful, Bess served as a center of gravity among these disorderly neighbors, but turned sharply inward after her husband's early death. Gornick grew up to become a writer and a feminist who lived alone in Greenwich Village, an alien in her mother's world. In *Fierce Attachments*, mother and adult daughter speed-walk furiously around the city, arguing about the possibilities for women's lives.

For the past five decades, Gornick has examined the conditions of women's entrapment and the possibility of their freedom. Less stylish but more immediate than her contemporary Joan Didion, and famously testy in interviews, she is a roving feminist critic cherished for her commitment to dissatisfaction. Ten years before *Fierce Attachments,* her breakthrough success, Gornick made a first attempt at writing about her youth in the Bronx. Published in 1977, her book *The Romance of American Communism* was a passionate, unwieldy auto-ethnographic work that zoomed out from her own upbringing to encompass the everyday life of the Communist Party in the United States. Initially scorned by critics and long out of print, it has recently become a cult classic among younger leftists and was reissued by Verso this spring.

The Romance of American Communism opens in Gornick's childhood apartment, this time bathed in a soft, hazy light. In *Fierce Attachments* the building must generate its own claustrophobic melodrama, but in *Romance* the outside is always pouring in. Immigrant workers congregated regularly in Gornick's parents' kitchen to eat black bread with herring and debate politics in Yiddish. Only some were party members, but all were part of the party's orbit, and it linked them

in solidarity with workers everywhere. In her house-
hold, the fact that "Papa worked hard all day long"—he
pressed clothes in a dress factory—was spoken with
reverence; the rest of the family was asked to identify
with his toil, perhaps in some ways not so differently
from how patriarchs are revered in more conservative
households. But solidarity also had the power, dramatic if fleeting, to blur other lines of division. "Before
I knew that I was Jewish or a girl," Gornick writes in
the book's astonishing first line, "I knew that I was a
member of the working class."

This world came to an end in 1956, Gornick
explains at the outset of *Romance*, when Nikita
Khrushchev denounced Stalin's atrocities against the
people of the Soviet Union and thousands of members, already strained by state persecution, left the
Communist Party within weeks. Gornick, then a City
College student living at home but drifting away from
the party, became numb to politics. She spent much
of the 1960s in Berkeley in an unhappy marriage and
unfocused graduate school career, marching only rotely
for civil rights and against the war in Vietnam. Then,
in 1969—divorced, dropped out, and back in New York
working as a reporter for the *Village Voice*—she discovered feminism. The *Voice* sent her to cover a group

of women's liberationists, including future luminaries Shulamith Firestone and Kate Millett, living together in Greenwich Village; she was skeptical at first, then consumed. "Within a week I was a convert," she said several years ago in an interview. "Feminism was like lightning. It went right through me."

Gornick was among the many children of communists who found a home within the new social movements of the 1960s and 1970s. Conservatives often accused young people who burned their draft cards or smoked marijuana of engaging in an oedipal revolt against their parents' values, but they brought the opposite charge against "'second-generation' radicals," indicting them for carrying on subversive family traditions. Rather than instigating "normal parent-child conflict," an article in the campus conservative magazine *Young Guard* argued in 1964, such radicals were "reiterating for the millionth time parental doctrines learned from the cradle." Sometimes this sort of messaging backfired; student organizers at University of California, Berkeley, for instance, received a windfall of useful recruitment data when the John Birch Society published a list of students from communist families. During her own stint at Berkeley, Gornick, removed for the first time from a working-class immigrant milieu, discovered that her political heritage was shocking to her new peers, who "thought of Communists as the nameless, faceless evil from across the sea." Angered and confused, she responded by bringing up her family's affiliations whenever possible, "exactly as I would have announced my Jewishness in the presence of open anti-Semitism." She also began to wonder if she should write about her communist childhood. Where had she come from, and what had she taken with her?

Gornick tells this origin story in a new introduction to *The Romance of American Communism,* and it says much about the volume that emerged. Fundamentally, the book—Gornick's second—is an attempt to make sense of a child's enchanted universe in a world that has subsequently been destroyed, and to recover it through the romantic pursuit of oral history. In doing so, she traces a path from what she calls the "ingrown world" of the leftists among whom she grew up to the far-flung comrades of their lore: communists from Cleveland, communists from Hollywood. "Secretly, I think I had always believed along with J. Edgar Hoover that the Communists were all New York Jews of Eastern European origin," Gornick writes. Researching the book, however, she discovered "that something I had been taught all my young life but had never actually believed was, in fact, *true*: the Communists had come from everywhere." She interviewed dozens of older communists and (more often) ex-communists around the country, and devotes most of *Romance* to telling their stories.

A different writer might have used this material in the service of a conventional social history, exploring the strategies communists adopted to briefly gain a modicum of power in the United States. But Gornick was more interested in the prefigurative aspect of political organizing, in which action in the present serves not just as a step toward change in the future, but also as a model for that change. *The Romance of American Communism* asks how it was that thousands of Americans saw their lives transformed by the Communist Party. Despite their often desperate material circumstances and the drudgery of much rank-and-file party organizing—"years of selling the *The Daily Worker*, running off mimeographed leaflets, speaking on street corners, canvassing door-to-door for local and national votes"—they repeatedly echo Richard Wright, whose verdict Gornick cites early in the book: "There was no agency in the world so capable of making men feel the earth and the people upon it as the Communist Party."

There is Dick Nikowsski, a slaughterhouse worker in Chicago radicalized the hot summer day a socialist

coworker tells him that the plant's owners are vaca-
tioning at the beach; he suddenly flashes upon his own
image, "knee-deep in blood and shit all my life so that
that picture could be taken," and understands that
because he can now see himself clearly, he can also
refuse to accept what he sees. There is Will Barnes,
born in a mining camp in Idaho, who witnesses the
massacre of the Wobblies in Centralia, Washington,
and is converted to communism by a charismatic sailor
when he ships out to sea. There is Blossom Sheed, who
migrates with her family from Memphis to Los Angeles and marries a cousin at 17. She cannot stop asking
why so many people are poor, but her husband refuses
to engage with the question. She eventually leaves him
and their child and joins the cooperative movement,
a Depression-era network of worker and consumer
collectives; then, seeing the cooperators perpetually
thwarted by capitalists, she joins the communists and
rises to become the secretary-general of a party-run
legal defense fund for striking farmworkers. There is
Marian Moran, the daughter of leftist intellectuals
in California who comes of age living and organizing
with fruit pickers on strike in the Imperial Valley and
goes on to serve for twenty-five years as a state party
chairwoman. "I've had three husbands, slept with more

men than I can count, borne children, had political power," Moran tells Gornick. "Of all the emotions I've known in life, nothing compares with the emotion of total comradeship I knew among the fruit pickers in the Thirties."

Inverting the old suspicions about Sovietized pod people, Gornick describes the American communists as being "like everybody else, only more so." It is precisely the "humanizing" quality of their politics, she argues, that makes their failure to recognize Soviet authoritarianism so tragic. In the aftermath of Khrushchev's de-Stalinization speech, Gornick was horrified at the idea of remaining in the party, her aunt was furious with her for leaving, and her grief-stricken mother could not decide. "We alone remained—we three women—in this crumbling house to face the crumbling world outside the kitchen," Gornick writes, and "stared at each other, each of us trapped in her own anguish." Decades later, their arguments float back to her in dreams, and seem to have informed an understanding of politics she has returned to throughout her life. In her 2005 book, *The Solitude of Self,* she recalls attending a lecture by the liberal Israeli novelist David Grossman at which an audience member asked Grossman why Israeli youth had not risen up against their country's rightward march. Grossman seemed nervous, "then burst out, 'We cannot bear to alienate ourselves from our parents,'" Gornick writes. "Everyone in the room could feel his anxiety. In that moment I understood my own country better."

Many characters in *The Romance of American Communism* describe losing their political innocence twice—first, when they joined the party, and second, when they left it. The power of their testimony comes in part from their insistence that the latter experience has complicated rather than undone the transformations wrought by the former. But despite the complexity of feeling Gornick records, the book's child's-eye view gave critics an opportunity to recycle old claims about the infantilism of the Communist Party. They were responding, perhaps, to the way that *Romance* preserves a Bronx accent—not a lyrical neighborhood voice like the ones Grace Paley channels in her stories about working-class New York Jews, but a searching, elevated descendant of the sound in Ethel Rosenberg's earnest, autodidactic letters. Like his contemporary Leslie Fiedler, Irving Howe spent the early years of the cold war railing against the popular front's "political baby talk." Decades later, he wrote of Gornick, "One sometimes has to remind oneself that in her evocation

of coziness and warmth she is writing about the CP
in the time of Stalin and not about a summer camp."
And yet by the time *Romance* was published, the few
remaining summer camps built by communists for
their children in the early 20th century had already
long survived the collapse of the party.

IT IS POSSIBLE THAT Haimie, my father's father, was a
socialist like some of the men he played with in a man-
dolin band, but we don't know because he didn't talk
much. In Leeds and then in Los Angeles he worked in a
paintbrush factory, sorting bristles; ever since Poland,
there had been rich Brostoffs who owned the brush
factories and poor Brostoffs who labored in them, and
he was among the latter. There were agitators at the
factory, and my grandma, Freda, was always after him
to join them. At the very least she wanted him to ask
for a raise, because he made $1.50 an hour. He would
yell at her to leave him alone; he was a very quiet man.
His passivity enraged her. Later he got Parkinson's.
Freda thought it was from the chemicals at the factory.
He died of it, but he was old by then, and his children
had long been comfortably middle class.

My mother's father, Lou, grew up in a tiny railroad
town in Saskatchewan called Pennant. Lou's father,

Max, had come from Bessarabia and settled near Sioux land in South Dakota before heading north to Pennant and opening a general store. The town has a mythic status in the family imagination, our own private nationalism, of which my mother is the keeper. She has lived in the suburbs of Los Angeles all her life, but she is a sort of gemeinschaft of one; wherever she goes, a little town appears. She traipses around the Valley, helping out: a bris in the morning, a bar mitzvah in the afternoon, a wedding in the evening, a funeral at night. I thought of her when I read the way the Christian socialist Frances Willard, leader of the Women's Christian Temperance Union in the late 19th century, described the purpose of her organization: "It is to make the whole world homelike." Both my parents are Democrats, and Zionists, like almost everyone around them.

I stopped arguing with my parents about Israel sometime in my early twenties. My mother in particular is a difficult person to disagree with. She is a woman who does not use a tape measure; her feet, she claims, each measure exactly one foot. Our fights had been exhausting and gotten us nowhere, so we learned to talk past each other. Neither of us had any desire to be marginal or besieged; we each wanted to be embedded in a transparently righteous social world, and tried to create hegemony through sheer force of personality. She would tell me whom she had run into at the Israel march that day and I would tell her about my afternoon at the Palestine rally. Because we lived on opposite sides of the country, there was no chance of running into each other.

Once, when my parents were visiting, I broke this tacit compact on a drive to Philadelphia with my mother and her cousin Janet. Janet and her son had been in a heated email exchange about whether Israel was an apartheid state, and then, she said, his emails had simply stopped coming. "Well, and so we shall cease to speak of such things, and our generation shall rise," I snapped from the back seat, like I was suddenly the Bible or something. Everyone was quiet; it isn't nice to tell people they will be swept away by time.

I was living that year with my boyfriend in a middle-income public housing complex around the block from the Grand Street co-ops, and we were on our way to breaking up. I came back from Philadelphia and he still hadn't cleaned the house, so I packed a bag and trudged across Delancey Street, under the Williamsburg Bridge, to Hillman. My mother rolled her eyes and said I couldn't run home crying every time I was having relationship problems, a peculiar complaint since they were only there for the week. I understood then the power of the Grand Street apartment: it was a bargain-basement time machine that transported us to Vivian Gornick's New York. Within its force field, every argument we had once, we seemed to have been rehashing for a hundred years.

AMERICANS LEARNED ABOUT Jewish mothers from Gertrude Berg, a radio and then television star whose alter ego, Molly Goldberg, was a national darling from the Great Depression until the McCarthy period. *The Goldbergs*—in its TV iteration it is sometimes described as the first sitcom—followed Molly and her clan through the daily adventures of Bronx tenement life: airshaft hijinks, surprise visitors. Molly was a "talkative busybody, a balaboste, but one with a loving heart," the cultural historian Joyce Antler writes, "who solved all the problems of her family, neighborhood, and community through her skillful 'mixing-in.'" The next Jewish woman to attract this kind of popular attention, Antler notes, was Ethel Rosenberg, who was widely portrayed as Molly's inverse: alien, unnatural, a bad mother. Berg—like Ethel, a theatrically inclined New York daughter of immigrants—studiously kept politics off the air in an attempt to keep the specter of the second Jewish mother from tarnishing the first, but she did not entirely succeed. She ran in leftist circles and may have been blacklisted; she was ultimately pressured into firing her television husband, the communist actor Philip Loeb, who killed himself a few years later. And yet even as the figure of Ethel Rosenberg threatened the image of Molly Goldberg, Molly would not last long in her tenement in the absence of Ethel's commitment to cooperative living. In the last seasons of *The Goldbergs*, filmed the years following the execution of the Rosenbergs, the family moves to the suburbs, where Molly is lonely.

In the 1970s, as public housing was decimated across the country, Julius and Ethel Rosenberg reappeared in a wave of literature and art. Adrienne Rich was haunted by Ethel's thwarted ambitions—Ethel took acting classes at the Lower East Side settlement house and met Julius singing choral music at a fundraiser for the International Seamen's Union—and by her mother's cruelty toward her. She wonders in an elegy whether Ethel, if she'd lived, would have eventually moved out and gotten her own apartment. Other writers reimagined the experiences of the Rosenbergs' children, excavating the recent fortunes of the

American left in the form of the family saga. In E. L. Doctorow's scorching 1971 novel, *The Book of Daniel,* Julius and Ethel become Paul and Rochelle Isaacson, Bronx communists executed after their closest comrade rats them out to the FBI. The horrific betrayal and loss forces their children into lives of total involution. Their son, Daniel, grows up to nurse his sexual fixation on his sister, Susan; Susan herself longs so ardently for the grave that she starts a nonprofit, the Paul and Rochelle Isaacson Foundation for Revolution.

The communist family in these stories is a fortress and a prison. No one gets out—and just as importantly, no one gets in. Who would understand, who could be trusted? Unable to reproduce, possessed by an inflamed partial recall of historical events drummed out of popular memory, communist families appear in red diaper family sagas as branches of a dying aristocracy. There is always someone trying ineptly to marry in or otherwise penetrate the family's walls, as though a gas burner left on in an apartment were a carefully guarded flame. If we have run out of hope, let us retreat, catalog our losses, let us study arcana, assemble in public at times of escalated crisis, let us seek out traces of holiness, let us remember that we exist. The plot of every Jewish holiday. I started working on this essay nearly five years ago, and stopped because I could not bear the shame of being homesick for diaspora and its cramped families, when other people had real problems.

The shame, the shame. In 1976, a year before *The Romance of American Communism* came out, Irving Howe published *World of Our Fathers,* a thick best seller about the history of Jewish socialists in the United States. The most meaningful distinction between the books—the distinction that allowed Howe to accuse Gornick of reducing Stalinism to summer camp—is not the distinction between the socialist and communist movements in the United States, but the fact that *Romance* is so plainly about the world of Gornick's mother. There is the unnamed schoolteacher who laughs and tells Gornick, "The Party was down on Freud, but in the Bronx we said, 'Yeah, yeah, but your mother's important, anyway.'" There is Sarah Gordon, another Jewish woman from the Bronx, who says,

> I used to envy people who had come into the movement in adult life. I used to think: What a thrill it must be for people to *discover* Marxism, to discover the Party. Me, there'd never been a moment in my conscious life when the Party wasn't there. There was Mama, there

> was Papa, there was the Party. I couldn't tell where one
> left off and the other began. Especially, I couldn't tell
> where my father left off and the Party began. . . . If my
> mother had ever wanted to sue for divorce she'd have
> had to name the Communist Party as correspondent.

There is Bess Gornick herself, in her kitchen, animating the communist horizon for her children as though prefigurative politics were just another term for reproductive labor. "He is a writer. She is a poet. He is a thinker," Gornick recalls her mother whispering in Yiddish when she asked about the comrades gathered in their home; only later did she come to understand that "*he*, of course, drove a bakery truck. *She* was a sewing-machine operator." The men in these stories walk out the door and disappear into the party; the women leave the door open and the party disappears into them. I wish Gornick had been able to picture Bess simultaneously as the whispering communist homemaker of *Romance* and the aching furious neighbor of *Fierce Attachments*. Between these images lies the possibility of a real reckoning with her mother as a subject.

Gornick took the poor reception of *Romance* to heart and came to see the book as a failure; even her

new introduction decries it as defensive and overwrit-
ten. Her new fans on the left appear to puzzle her.
And yet—perhaps because, like the sphinx of Thebes,
she is implacable and looks like both a woman and a
cat—she seems to get into a lot of conversations with
young wanderers searching for their real parents. The
volume's new edition, she writes, is for them:

> Today, the idea of socialism is peculiarly alive, especially
> among young people in the United States, in a way it
> has not been for decades. Yet today there is no exist-
> ing model in the world of a socialist society to which
> a young radical can hitch a star or a truly international
> organization to which she or he can pledge. Socialists
> today must build their own unaffiliated version of how
> to achieve a more just world from the bottom up. It is
> my hope that *Romance*, telling the story of how it was
> done some sixty or seventy years ago, can act as a guide
> to those similarly stirred today.

WE SAT AROUND THE TABLE at the Grand Street apartment. I thought my parents might not want to be interviewed about anything political, but when I turned on
the tape recorder they opened up right away, as though
we were merely reminiscing about the past. "I had my

own socialist experience," my mother said. She lived
for a few months on a kibbutz near Acre, in northwest
Israel, in 1972. She picked pears and worked in the
chicken coops in exchange for room, board, and $5 a
week. Her roommates were Russians—it was the time
of the first big Soviet migration to Israel—and one day
when they didn't want to work they made big signs
declaring themselves on strike. My mother suggested
that they come up with a demand, so they demanded
more cigarettes. The strike failed and they went back
to work. Once she was hitchhiking and a young Palestinian man picked her up and for a while he became
her boyfriend. She didn't know he was Palestinian; the
kibbutzniks had to tell her. She stayed in the country
for nearly a year, and then she went home.

I asked what it meant to her that the kind of socialism practiced on the kibbutz was for Jews only, that the
collective farms were built on top of other people's bull-
dozed towns. "We didn't hear about taking over lands,"
she said. Then, she reflected, "Probably I was taught
some of this and I wasn't paying attention. Did my heart
connect to something unrealistically because I didn't
know the darker side? And at the same time there was
something very passionate and beautiful about having
a connection to this homeland. I thought people would

be doing Israeli dances in the street. It was this culture I had grown up with—Israeli song, dance, food—that was like, 'Wow, this is a Jewish place.'"

"We have a romance with Israel," said my dad. We had been talking about Israel for so long, after so many years, that I almost forgot to ask them how they were feeling about the return of the left in American politics. "I have no problem with the rise in socialist ideals in the United States," he said. "I have a lot of problems with the anti-Israel baggage that goes with it." When I asked him about climate change, he said he was glad he'd be dead by then.

It became increasingly difficult, last year, to pretend that we agreed on much at all. I had given up on trying to be a woman and was working on becoming something else instead; my parents seemed to see my refusal to be a daughter as a refusal to be their child, another attempt to replace them. Israel and Palestine, the terms we had always used to contain our other disagreements, seeped out and were everywhere now. When I walked through my neighborhood in Brooklyn, I tried to hold its weathered stately architecture in my mind in case it should all come crashing down in a war. My friends and I tried our best to explain to our elders that uncooperative living was not safe, but unlike the American communists, the

American Democrats did not think much about what their party had given them—a conception of space and time—until it started to break down.

No one really wanted to turn the recorder off, but it was getting late; my parents were heading up to visit friends in Westchester before returning to LA, and I was heading back to Brooklyn. They rolled their suitcases out to the curb and I hailed them a cab. I had thought I wanted to betray them, but it turned out I just wanted to talk to them, and when I left, I didn't want to leave them.

IN NEW YORK, a snowless winter came. Our side was up in the national polls, and a sense of giddiness took hold, as though everyone were playing house, practicing for a new world that might or might not arrive. I dreamed my dad and I were arguing about health care in the Soviet Union, a topic on which we were equally ignorant. I woke up to myself mocking him for asking what was even the point of redesigning our medical system, given that nothing could be known about anything. "Sure!" I yelled. "Why are there camels? Why is there the sea?" In real life he told me he was thinking about voting for Amy Klobuchar in the California primaries, and I burst out laughing as though I had nothing to lose.

Then a few weeks passed and the climate changed. Sirens enclosed my neighborhood in a barrier of sound. Once, early in the isolation period, I walked all the way down the hill to the Walgreens on Fulton Street. Cops patrolled a line that stretched hygienically, beneath the filthy scaffolding, from the subway to the store. Inside, a tired pharmacist in a mask told me my insurance had no record of a prescription it normally covered every month, so I wandered the empty aisles, past shelves of aspirin and mascara, arranged pitifully beneath a former bank's domed ceiling like cough drops at the bottom of a purse, until I was allowed to pay out of pocket. After that I did my best to stay in the relative countryside up the hill, leaving home only for the market and the little park next to our house, where police cars still circled lazily but new buds kept opening indifferently overhead. After a month I broke quarantine and walked down the street to a friend's. Our other friend walked over from a different part of Brooklyn. We sat on the roof and looked at the fearsome Manhattan skyline absurdly far away. By the end of the night it was like we were all related.

My building is not very tall but it is wide, with wings folding out from the lobby like a parliament. Legally speaking it is a co-op; our landlord converted it in the 1990s in a real estate ploy, then bought and sublet nearly all the shares. When quarantine began, the world shrank to the building's size and everyone became a mad housewife in their cabin fever. There were frenzies in the tenant WhatsApp thread: a package thief, tacos for 2L abandoned in the lobby. Chimney swifts were spotted on the roof of the haunted 19th-century institutional building—now a Seventh Day Adventist school, someday slated to be dwarfed by condos—across the street. Once someone saw turkey vultures. "Sure it wasn't management?" someone else asked. It became clear that if rent continued to drain from the apartments, the neighborhood would wash away. We formed a committee and slipped flyers under doors. They came back covered in complaints. Upstairs a patch of black mold was growing in a baby's room; it measured less than a square foot, so the housing inspectors couldn't be bothered. I desperately wanted to learn everyone's problems and names.

I fantasized at first that organizing my building would be a chance to prove my masculinity, but soon I realized that I had once again become my mother. In California, she canceled cousin Shaindie's 100th birthday party, but bragged that she'd still dropped off deli sandwiches. I boasted back that I'd bought groceries for an old lady I didn't even know. I gabbed on the phone with neighbors for hours a day, loading and unloading the dishwasher, telling the same stories over and over. There was a death in the family in 4M and I brought flowers; 6J brought me strawberry biscuits. My mother helped plan a Zoom bat mitzvah. In my building, we withheld the rent.

There was Selma Gardinsky, a red diaper baby from Brooklyn transplanted to Boston by marriage, where she took a unionized office job and became an organizer in an attempt to catch the party's eye. She left her husband "without so much as a backward glance" when the union offered her a position back in New York; there, she was recruited by the Communist Party and went to work for it for "the best ten years" of her life. "Whatever else we were or were not as Communists," Gardinsky told Gornick, "we were not lonely." There was Bernie Sanders, a socialist from a Brooklyn immigrant family who does not appear in *Romance*. He became the mayor of a small city in Vermont, then a senator, and finally ran twice for President. "I have cast some lonely votes, fought some lonely fights, mounted some lonely campaigns," he wrote in 2015. "But I do not feel lonely now." I don't feel lonely anymore, but it isn't nearly enough.

An infinite amount of care seems necessary. While we gather our strength, the lucky ones among us will grow old.

ACKNOWLEDGMENTS

"WHERE THE BOYS ARE," "MISSING TIME," AND "THE FAMILY Romance of American Communism" previously appeared in *n+1*, where Dayna Tortorici and Mark Krotov—who has also seen this book through from conception to production—taught me the art of editing through their brilliant example. "The Double's Allegiance" appeared in Post45, thanks to the guidance of Len Gutkin. "The Right Kind of Continuity" first appeared in *Jewish Currents*, where it emerged from conversations with coworkers including Noah Kulwin, who cowrote the piece, and Arielle Angel, who edited it. The book took on material form thanks also to the extraordinary designs of Rachel Ossip and the contagious enthusiasm of Lisa Borst.

Much of this book was written while I was finishing graduate school, and owes a great deal to the academic coconspirators and mentors who read or talked through versions of these essays at the time, including Sarah Chihaya, James Duesterberg, Jules Gill-Peterson,

Leon Hilton, Wayne Koestenbaum, Summer Kim Lee, Eric Lott, Lakshmi Padmanabhan, Iván Ramos, Dan Sinykin (who later directly oversaw the book's completion, as in sat with me at a bar while I finished final edits), Alyson Spurgas, JT Tremblay, and everyone in Stanley Aronowitz's reading group. Special thanks are due to Andrea Long Chu, Nancy K. Miller, and Ethan Philbrick, who in various ways gave me permission to turn my academic research into a different mode of writing and thinking. My parents, Marlene and Neal Brostoff, generously agreed to be interviewed for the book's final essay and lent their support throughout the process. *Missing Time* was completed over the first year of the pandemic, and I thank the friends with whom I spent the quarantine period for keeping me intact, including my dear podmates Dan Drake, Allison Hughes, and Peter Oleksik, as well as my far-flung comrades Alex Colston, Alex Press, and Gabe Winant, who read or offered moral support on the introduction. Tracy Jeanne Rosenthal arrived on the scene toward the end of the process and changed the texture of time completely.

Two important teachers, Stanley Aronowitz and Lauren Berlant, died shortly before the publication of this book. May their memory be a blessing.